TWO ESSAYS ON

For John H.
with fondest regards

John P.

TWO ESSAYS ON VIRGIL

Intertextual Issues in *Aeneid* 6 and *Georgics* 4

JOHN PENWILL

Studies in Western Traditions
Occasional Papers No. 2

Department of Humanities
La Trobe University, Bendigo
1995

Studies in Western Traditions
Occasional Papers in the Humanities

There is only the fight to recover what has been lost
And found and lost again and again

T.S. Eliot

Publisher:
Department of Humanities, School of Arts, La Trobe University, P O Box 199, Bendigo, Victoria, Australia 3550.
Tel: (054) 44 7237 or (054) 44 7234   Fax: (054) 44 7970
E-mail: J.Penwill@bendigo.latrobe.edu.au

Editorial Panel:
Rodney Blackhirst, Harry Oldmeadow, John Penwill, Sara Warneke.

Advice to potential contributors:
This series exists to provide a format for work in the traditional Humanities disciplines which is longer than the average journal article but shorter than the average monograph—that is to say roughly in the range of 7,000 to 20,000 words. Contributions comprising two or more essays on a common theme by a single author or group of authors are also accepted. Submissions should be typed in double spacing and supplied both in hard copy and on disk (WordPerfect 6.1 or Microsoft Word 5.0 preferred). The text of the hard copy should contain no indication of the identity of the author. Please direct submissions to a member of the Editorial Panel at the publisher's address above: note, however, that while contributions are welcome no responsibility can be accepted for unsolicited material.

© Dept of Humanities, La Trobe University, Bendigo 1995
ISBN 0 909977 20 8

CONTENTS

INTRODUCTION

> ...The most important component of the literary work
> of art, and indeed the key to the interpretation of its
> significance, should be found outside that work, beyond
> its margins, in the intertext.
>
> Michael Riffaterre

ONE aspect of Virgil's work that instantly strikes the reader is
the extent of his use of material from earlier writers.[1] The
simplistic response to this was to say that in the *Eclogues* Virgil
was setting himself up as the Roman Theocritus, in the *Georgics*
the Roman Hesiod, and in the *Aeneid* the Roman Homer. The
philhellenic nineteenth century, whose motto as far as Roman
literature was concerned was Horace *Epistles* 2.1.156f,[2] saw this
as the prime example justifying their reductive view that Roman
culture was merely an extension or adaptation of Greek. The
poem that took over from Ennius' *Annales* as Rome's national
epic could now be seen as nothing more than an inferior
imitation of the *Iliad* and the *Odyssey*; and besides, even Ennius
had depicted himself as the Roman Homer and chosen to force
his Latin into the Greek hexameter, thus acknowledging that the
only way to celebrate Roman political and military achievement
was by rendering it in Homeric epic narrative.

---

[1] A useful account of the history of the treatment of Virgilian intertextuality
may be found in Farrell (1991), 3-25.

[2] *Graecia capta ferum uictorem cepit et artes/intulit agresti Latio* ('Greece
taken captive took captive her fierce conqueror and brought the arts to
rustic Latium'). The peroration of Anchises' speech at *Aen.*6.847-53 could
also be adduced in support of this position, since poetry is conspicuously
absent in what are to be the *artes* of the Romans.

1

The position has now radically changed. Virgilian allusion is recognised as far more wideranging (even nineteeth century *Quellenforschung* had demonstrated that) and subtle than this earlier simplistic view had suggested. It encompasses not only Greek authors but also Roman, and not only poets but also philosophers and historians; in Virgil's text we find allusions to Homer, Hesiod, Euripides, Plato, Aristotle, Apollonius, Callimachus, Theocritus, Aratus, Ennius, Lucretius, Catullus, Varro, Cicero, and himself, to name but a selection of the more significant. And it is *functional*; that is to say, Virgil generates meaning in his text through these allusions. They constitute a deliberate intertextual framework which not only imparts the appropriate flavour to the Virgilian text but also—and more importantly—itself generates meaning in that text. Intertextuality is an integral part of Virgilian signification. And this is a feature of Roman literature that is not confined to Virgil. Born out of an awareness of an essential Romanness in Roman literature even as it was experimenting with the adaptation of Greek forms (the relationship between the first line of Livius Andronicus' *Odussia* and Homer's *Odyssey* is instructive),[3] the art of functional allusion (or *arte allusiva* as Pasquali called it in a seminal article in 1942)[4] reached its full flowering in the work of poets and prose writers in the first century BCE and remained an important characteristic of Roman poetry thereafter. More recent critics, following Julia Kristeva's coinage of the term,[5]

---

[3] On which see Goldberg (1993), 22f.

[4] On Pasquali's doctrine of *arte allusiva* see Farrell (1991), 11-13, and Conte (1986), 24-28.

[5] On the history of this term and the manifestation of the phenomenon in classical and post-classical literature and literary theory, see Still & Worton (1991), 1-44, with bibliography there cited.

call this functional allusion intertextuality and talk of 'intertextual relationships'. These exist—and importantly exist—in the work of Catullus (with e.g. Homer, Sappho, Callimachus, Lucilius), Lucretius (with e.g. Homer, Empedocles, Thucydides, Epicurus, Ennius, Lucilius, Catullus) and Cicero (whose *De Re Publica* has an overt, close and functional relationship with Plato's *Politeia*).[6] Such intertextual relationships with not just Greek but also earlier and even near-contemporary Roman authors is evidence of a growing sense among writers of the period that they are part of a tradition which combines both Greek and Roman. It is a tradition that we have come to call classical.

Despite important recent work in this field by Virgilian scholars such as Gransden (1984), Boyle (1986), Conte (1986), Thomas (1986) and Farrell (1991), there is still a tendency on the part of classicists, particularly in the British tradition, to talk in terms of 'imitation' and 'influence' rather than 'allusion' and 'intertextuality'. The title given to the collection of essays edited by West and Woodman, *Creative Imitation and Latin Literature*, is symptomatic here.[7] It may be objected that the ancients themselves recognised only two ways in which a later author might engage with the work of an earlier, these being *imitatio* and *aemulatio*;[8] but the fact that this was the way they perceived the issue does not mean that we have no alternative but to follow them. One of the hallmarks of great literature is

---

[6] Cf. Penwill (1994), 70ff.; on the title of Plato's work, see below p.13 n.8.
[7] West & Woodman (1979).
[8] 'Longinus' 13.2-14.3; Quintilian 10.1.122. See Russell (1979) *passim*; and cf. West & Woodman (1979), 200: 'The word "imitation"...in its Latin form is firmly embedded in the writings of ancient literary critics and there is now no way of dispensing with it.'

that it transcends the limited and limiting classifications of pedestrian critics and theorists; even the presence of a towering intellect like Aristotle does not impede us from approaching Athenian tragedy directly rather than refracted through the prism of the *Poetics*. We approach and interpret these works employing the critical methodologies of our own age; we can do no other.[9] And works of the calibre of what we have come to call 'classics' will appear all the richer for this treatment.

It is an obvious truism that Virgil was writing for an educated readership, one which would recognise the intertextual aspect of his poetry. Responses might merely take the form of turning the act of reading into a game of 'spot the allusion', a Barthesian 'cruising' through the texts looking for intertextual 'erotic sites'.[10] It is clear, however, that Virgil expects more of his reader than engaging in this kind of 'trivial pursuit'. His work demands an intelligent, sensitive and perceptive readership, not just a well-read one; one in fact that is both equipped and willing to probe the text for meaning, and capable of recognising that intertextual allusion is part of Virgil's strategy for constructing that meaning.

The two essays in this volume explore ways in which intertextuality functions in Virgil's text as a means of inviting a particular response to the events narrated or the ideological

---

[9] This of course is the issue that underlies Borges' well-known story 'Pierre Menard, Author of the *Quixote*'. See esp. Borges (1970), 65-71, where the question of how we read texts from the past is treated with characteristic Borgesian wit.

[10] 'Or finally: the text itself, a diagrammatic and not an imitative structure, can reveal itself in the form of a body, split into fetish objects, into erotic sites', Barthes (1982), 410 (from *The Pleasure of the Text*). On the image of the reader as *dragueur* in Barthes, cf. Knight (1990), 104f. Horsfall (1981) envisages the intended relation between Virgil's reader and Virgil's text to be of such a kind, in which recognition is the primary aim.

position advanced. They were both originally delivered as papers in the Pacific Rim Roman Literature Seminar series, the first at the University of Sydney in July 1994 (where the theme was 'The Ethical Imperative: Philosophy and Literature in Rome') and the second at the Villa Caproni, Temple University's Rome campus, in June 1995 (theme: *Urbs Poetica*: The Idea and Image of Rome in Imperial Literature').[11] I count myself fortunate to be a foundation member of this series which started at the University of Tasmania in 1987 and has continued on an annual basis ever since; the combination of convivial collegiality and rigorous debate which characterises these seminars has been particularly valuable as a reminder of what the study of the humanities is all about.

---

[11] The essays are printed here in the order in which they were delivered, which accounts for what may seem to some an illogical arrangement.

CHAPTER 1

MYTHS, DREAMS AND MYSTERIES

Intertextual Keys to *Aeneid* 6

> And be these juggling fiends no more believed
> That palter to us in a double sense;
> That keep the word of promise to our ear
> But never to our hope.
> > (Shakespeare, *Macbeth* 5.8.19-22)

WHEN Odysseus is told by Circe in Book 10 of the *Odyssey* that he must journey to the realm of the dead, he is devastated:

> So she spoke, and the inward heart within me was broken,
> and I sat down on the bed and cried, nor did the heart in me
> wish to go on living any longer, nor to look on the sun-
> light.[1]

When Aeneas is given the same instruction by the dream-image of his father Anchises towards the end of *Aeneid* 5, however, we find a very different response. The only anguish he displays is at the fact that his father's image recedes from his consciousness; the instruction he proceeds to follow eagerly and without question. The man of *pietas* can do no other; as soon as he lands at Cumae he seeks out the sibyl and, after dutifully following Helenus' instruction to consult her about the future (see 3.441-60), he delivers a speech whose purpose is to persuade her to enable him

---

[1]   *Odyssey* 10.496-98, tr. Lattimore (1968).

to descend into the underworld (6.106-23). The cardinal virtue which drives him forward is recognised by Anchises when they finally meet in the closing section of the book: *uicit iter durum pietas* ('*pietas* has overcome the difficult journey', 6.689).

In this, the climax of the Odyssean half of the *Aeneid*, Virgil follows his normal technique of setting up a complex of inter-textual relationships, the most immediately obvious being with the *Nekuia* of Homer's *Odyssey*; as Boyle points out in his essay on the *Aeneid* in the Routledge *Roman Epic*, the allusion is constant.[2] And the particular set of circumstances outlined above represents a good initial example of Virgil's use of intertextuality. In both the *Odyssey* and the *Aeneid*, the instruction to visit the realm of the dead comes when the hero seems to have lost his way: Odysseus has spent a year enjoying the pleasant company of Circe and has to be reminded by his crew that they ought to be thinking of getting home (*Od.* 10.472-4), while Aeneas has been in an agony of indecision about what to do in the face of the obvious disinclination of a significant number of his followers to continue travelling in search of a home (see esp. *Aen.* 5.700-04 and 719-20). In both cases the indecision has already been resolved (Odysseus has accepted the advice of his men and determined to resume his voyage, and Aeneas has been told by the dream-image of Anchises to accept Nautes' advice); in both cases the instruction to make the journey to Hades' comes right out of the blue; in both cases the purpose of this journey is to consult the shade of a particular individual about the future; and in both cases the instruction is given towards the end of the book prior to that in which the actual journey is narrated. And prior to embarking on this journey a death

---

[2]   Boyle (1993), 94-98.

occurs which will find a resonance in the journey itself: that of Elpenor in the *Odyssey* and that of Palinurus in the *Aeneid*.

Setting up these structural, narrative and thematic parallels of course serves to throw the differences into sharp relief and thus engage the reader's attention. I have already mentioned how Aeneas' *pietas* is emphasised by the different way in which he and Odysseus respond to the necessity of their journey; but there is another revealing character distinction highlighted here. Odysseus has himself made the decision to resume his voyage home as *Od.* 10.475 makes clear; it is he who requests Circe to allow him and his crew to depart, and it is in response to this that Circe announces that he must first make his voyage to the land of the dead. The anguish he displays is that of a man who sees this (understandably) as an appallingly frustrating interruption to the course of action he has decided upon. In the case of Aeneas, however, the instruction comes as the second of a pair delivered by Anchises with the endorsement of Jupiter (5.726f.); it relieves him of the task which he had been finding too much for him, that of having to think and make decisions for himself. It is as if he has opened another of the sealed envelopes that form his mission statement; he has no lack of courage in carrying out the instructions therein contained and proceeds unhesitatingly and single-mindedly so to do.[3] So we have on the one hand Odysseus πολύτροπος, deviser and implementer of stratagems; and on the other, Aeneas *pius*, the man who does what others tell him is his duty.

This crucial difference between Aeneas and Odysseus is high-lighted also in the Elpenor/Palinurus parallel. It is of course

---

[3]   Cf. Bishop (1988), 104: 'Gone are the anxieties, doubts and tensions: Aeneas is now the leader again and his behaviour is brisk and businesslike.' See also Heinze (1914), 275.

significant that whereas Odysseus is unaware of Elpenor's death until he encounters his shade in the land of the dead (see esp. *Od.* 11.55-58), Aeneas already thinks he knows about the fate of Palinurus and is therefore not surprised in the same way as Odysseus is when he meets him on the banks of the Styx. The issue for Aeneas is the fulfilment of prophecy and the trustworthiness of Apollo's oracle (6.341-46); Palinurus' reply to Aeneas' question *en haec promissa fides est?* ('is this how he [i.e. Apollo] fulfils his promise?') shows that both Aeneas and we are mistaken in thinking that Palinurus was drowned when he fell overboard at the end of Book 5, and thus in a technical sense the oracle that he would make it to Ausonia was fulfilled. That oracles can be fulfilled in this cruel and deceptive way (as Macbeth also discovered) should of course be a lesson to Aeneas (as to the reader) that oracles do not always mean what we expect them to mean—but that is another story. Here we should note the parallelism in the pleas made by Elpenor and Palinurus to their respective leaders to perform the appropriate funerary rites and the diametrically opposite response. Odysseus unhesitatingly promises to grant his dead comrade's request in a simple one-line reply (*Od.* 11.80), and the funeral of Elpenor is the first task to occupy him on his return to Aiaia (12.8-15). In the case of Palinurus on the other hand it is the sibyl who steps in to reply. Ignoring his plea for burial and concentrating only on his second request that Aeneas should take him with him over the Styx, the sibyl roundly attacks him for his presumption, concluding this part of her reply with the chilling words *desine fata deum flecti sperare precando* ('cease hoping that the fates decreed by the gods are swerved by prayer', 6.376). To Palinurus as to Misenus is offered the spurious compensation of the *aeternum nomen* in a local placename (381), a grotesque parody of the τύμβος and στήλη that mark the site of Elpenor's funeral, and one which gives joy not to the dead but to the land (*gaudet cognomine terra*, 'the land rejoices in its name', 383).[4] Palinurus was an expendable pawn, as the conclusion of Book 5 makes clear; to grant his request for burial now would impose an unacceptable delay on the mission. No room here for the obligation due to a dead comrade, and the sibyl steps in to ensure that any such feelings on Aeneas' part will be suppressed. It is Misenus who gets the Elpenor treatment of mound, arms, oar and trumpet, because the sibyl perceives in him a pollution that affects the whole enterprise (*totamque incestat funere classem*, 'and is polluting the entire fleet by his death', 150). Odysseus is free to make his own decisions based on his own moral sensibility; Aeneas cannot be permitted such a luxury at this crucial stage.

Virgil thus commences his account of Aeneas' journey through the underworld with an episode that carefully parallels Homer's narrative structure; Palinurus is the first individual encountered by Aeneas just as Elpenor is the first encountered by Odysseus. Thereafter, however, their paths diverge. Indeed, one can hardly talk of a path followed by Odysseus, since he remains on the

---

4   The MSS read *gaudet cognomine terrae*; the reading given is that of Servius, as adopted by Austin (1977). In his note on the passage, Austin insists on taking *terra* as ablative and *cognomine* as the ablative of the adjective *cognominis*, 'having the same name', translating 'and he takes delight in the land named after him'; cf. Day Lewis's (1966) 'in the joy of giving his name to a region'. But to make an unexpressed Palinurus the subject of *gaudet* involves a very harsh change of subject from *dolor* in the previous clause (particularly since Palinurus has not been the subject of a verb since *fatus erat* in line 372); it is more natural to take *cognomine* as the ablative of the noun *cognomen* (a much commoner word than the rare *cognominis*) and *terra* as nominative and subject of *gaudet*. That the other reading is possible gives the phrase an interesting ambiguity, but it is not the one that would occur to a first time reader—as the fact that it requires an extensive note to support it attests.

threshold waiting for the shades to come to him, whereas Aeneas actually travels through the realm of the dead to emerge finally in the Elysian fields. Furthermore, Virgil reverses the order of events to have Aeneas achieve the ostensible object of his journey at the end of it, whereas Odysseus gets the business part of his trip over with first. After he has consulted Teiresias, Odysseus becomes virtually a tourist, satisfying his intellectual curiosity by contemplating the shades of those who lived in previous generations and taking the opportunity to converse with his former comrades at Troy; the break in the middle of *Odyssey* 11 (330-84) which returns us to the palace of Alkinoos has something of the air of a returned traveller asking if his audience really wants to see any more of his holiday snapshots. Virgil's inversion of this narrative order turns Aeneas' encounters with Palinurus, Dido and Deiphobus and his general vision of the afterlife into a prelude to the final encounter with the shade who summoned him there rather than the incidental bonus of being able to decide that 'I might as well have a look round while I'm here'. The significance of this I shall discuss in a moment. Two other points first. One is the very different nature of the prophecies presented by Teiresias and Anchises. Teiresias only makes statements about the past: Odysseus' troubles are a direct consequence of his blinding the Cyclops Polyphemos. About the future he talks almost exclusively in conditional clauses of the kind that require subjunctives and optatives and a liberal sprinkling of potential particles; for him, as for Borges' Yu Tsun, the future is a labyrinthine garden of forking paths.[5] Anchises on the other hand shows no such linguistic hesitation: present and future indicatives characterise his foretelling of the future glory of Rome. Again one gets the sense that Odysseus' destiny is very

---

[5]   Borges (1970), 44-54.

much in his own hands while that of Aeneas and those who are descended from him is set in concrete, an inexorable chain of historical process leading from Aeneas to Caesar Augustus. The thought that Aeneas might choose to abandon the mission is at no stage entertained. And this leads to the second point. It is Odysseus who chooses when he has had enough and it is time to depart from the realm of the dead; in the case of Aeneas, the decision is made by Anchises (*Anchises...emittit*, 'Anchises sends them forth', 897f.). Again Virgil confronts us with the picture of a man who has surrendered control of his life to follow the dictates of *pietas*; a man in fact who is now living out the consequences of the choice he made at Carthage. The encounter with Dido earlier in Book 6, with its clear echoes of Odysseus' encounter with Ajax in *Odyssey* 11, tellingly underscores the distance between the two heroes.[6] Odysseus frankly wishes he had never won the contest which led to Ajax' suicide (ὡς δὴ μὴ ὄφελον νικᾶν τοιῷδ' ἐπ' ἀέθλῳ, 'would that I had not won in a contest of that kind', *Od.* 11.548); all Aeneas can do is reiterate his claim of 4.361 that he was acting against his inclination (*inuitus, regina, tuo de litore cessi*, 'it was against my will, O queen, that I left your shore', *Aen.* 6.460).[7] It is only Odysseus who when confronted with the consequences of his action proclaims that if he had his time over again he would act

---

6 For further discussion of the way in which this intertextual relationship determines our perception of Aeneas' response to Dido here, see Johnson (1976), 82-84.

7 This line of course sets up its own intertextual relationship with Catullus 66.39, where Berenice's lock states *inuita, o regina, tuo de uertice cessi* ('it was against my will, o queen, that I left your head'). The irony generated by having Aeneas thus evoke the discharge of a woman's vow on the safe return of her lover-husband (*pro dulci coniuge*, 33~*Aen.* 4.324) is poignant; certainly deserving of a more sensitive response than 'Catullus wasted a splendid line; Virgil shows how it can be put to better use' (Russell [1979], 13).

differently. Again, that is a luxury granted only to those whose lives are theirs to run.

As mentioned earlier, Virgil has deliberately and consciously (re)structured his narrative so that the prophetic passage comes as the climactic conclusion to the book. It is also obvious from even a superficial reading that the concluding section of *Aeneid* 6 is more 'philosophical' and more overtly ideological than what has gone before. What we find as we read Virgil's text more closely is that he is establishing another set of intertextual relationships, where the net is widened to draw in allusions to philosophic myth: particularly to Plato's 'Myth of Er' and to Cicero's 'Dream of Scipio', both mythic conclusions to large-scale works of political philosophy. Structurally the prophecy of Anchises (and in this I include his account of cosmology at 6.724ff.) functions as a mythic underpinning of the ideology implied in the first half of the poem, the goal towards which the odyssean wanderings of *Aeneid* 1-6 have been directed; the parallel to the structure of Plato's *Politeia*[8] and Cicero's *De Re Publica* is pointed and deliberate.

To take Plato first. The idea that we occupy a rational and moral universe in which virtue is rewarded and vice punished and the notion that souls have a pre-natal existence is central to both Socrates' and Anchises' world-view; the left-hand and right-hand paths for the wicked and just respectively occur at *Rep.* 614c and *Aen.* 6.540-43, and the thousand year journey during which souls experience the consequences of their actions in their previous

---

[8] A work whose traditional title is normally if misleadingly rendered in English as *Republic*, a Latin word which (as Cicero's work itself shows) has significantly different connotations from the Greek πολιτεία (= 'a socio-politico-legal system suitable for a πόλις'). I thus prefer to use the Greek title, although when abbreviating one is forced to use the Latin *Rep.* to avoid confusion with that other work of Plato's whose title is *not* conventionally Latinised, the *Politikos*.

incarnation is likewise common to both (*Rep.* 615a and *Aen.* 6.748). In both texts it is after the completion of this thousand-year cycle that souls assemble to be once again incarnated in a human body. But it is here that we encounter two crucial and fundamentally significant differences. In Plato souls are identified from their previous incarnations as we read of the lives chosen by those who were once Orpheus, Thamyris, Ajax, Agamemnon, Odysseus and others, and they use the experience of their previous incarnation in making their choice. In the *Aeneid* on the other hand souls are identified from the lives they are about to live; there is no opportunity for the exercise of choice or for learning from experience—a fact emphasised by the other crucial divergence Virgil makes, which is to have souls drink the water of forgetfulness *before* they are allotted a life (6.749-51), not, as in Plato, after.[9] Socrates' myth turns on the vital importance of equipping ourselves with the capacity to make the right moral choices, which is a matter of being able to see the consequences of adopting one course of action rather than another. Anchises' Romans have no such ability, a fact underscored by the futility of his appeal to the souls of Caesar and Pompey to refrain from civil war at 6.832-35. A moral system based on *pietas* and *mos maiorum* rather than insight into the true nature of things cannot in the end stand against the impulse towards personal aggrandisement and the pursuit of wealth and power; the choices made by the leading political figures of the last days of the Roman republic are those of the soul who chose the tyranny at *Rep.* 619b-d:

---

[9] Cf. Camps (1969), 88f. Camps notes this reverse order and other instances of discrepancy, but does not grasp the significance of these discrepancies for an understanding of Virgil's text.

And when the προφήτης[10] had spoken, he who had the first
choice came forward and in a moment chose the greatest
tyranny; his mind having been darkened by folly and
sensuality, he had not made any thorough inspection before
he chose, and did not perceive that he was fated, among
other evils, to devour his own children. But when he had
time to examine the life, he beat his breast and lamented
over his choice, forgetting the proclamation of the
προφήτης; for instead of blaming himself for his evils, he
accused chance and the gods and everything rather than
himself. Now he was one of those who came from heaven,
and in a former life had dwelt in a well-ordered πολιτεία;
his share of virtue derived from habit without philosophy.

(after Jowett)

ἔθος ἄνευ φιλοσοφίας, 'habit without philosophy'; for Plato the
weakness of the Spartan system, for Virgil that of the Roman.[11] So
it is with Aeneas: when his προφήτης, the sibyl, articulates for him
the consequences of the life he has chosen, that he will recreate the
Trojan War in Italy and that a second Achilles has already been
born (*alius Latio iam partus Achilles*, 6.89), he is, and remains,
unable to comprehend. As the poem moves through to the climax
of its Iliadic half, we see the devouring of children in the fates of

---

[10] Normally rendered 'Interpreter' (Cornford, Rouse, Lee), although Jowett has
'prophet'.

[11] One might note here the comparison of souls about to be reincarnated to bees
at *Aen.* 6.706ff., which invites reading in the light of Plato *Phaedo* 82b: 'I
suppose that the happiest people...are the ones who have cultivated the
goodness of an ordinary citizen...which is acquired by habit and practice,
without the help of philosophy and reason'—'How are these the happiest?'—
'Because they will probably pass into some other kind of social and
disciplined creature like bees, wasps, and ants...But no soul which has not
practised philosophy, and is not absolutely pure when it leaves the body, may
attain to the divine nature; that is only for the lover of learning.' (Tr.
Tredennick & Tarrant [1993], 141f.)

Nisus, Euryalus, Pallas, Lausus,[12] and the *alius Achilles* is revealed
by numerous unambiguous allusions to the *Iliad* as Aeneas himself.[13] Those who choose wisely, said Socrates' προφήτης, even
if they are last in line will find a life that is ἀγαπητός, 'desirable'
(*Rep.* 619b); for Aeneas and his companions on the other hand the
sibyl has this to say:

> in regna Lauini
> Dardanidae uenient (mitte hanc de pectore curam),
> sed non et uenisse uolent.
>
> *(Aeneid* 6.84-6)

The descendants of Dardanus will come to the kingdom of
Lavinium (cast this particular worry from your mind), but
they will also wish that they had not come.

They will get what they have chosen, but the consequences will
show that theirs was not a wise choice. If this is where *pietas*
leads, then *pietas* as a virtue is seriously flawed.

The 'Myth of Er' is evoked by geographical echoes and by the
motif of reincarnation; when we come to look at allusions to
Cicero's 'Dream of Scipio', we find they are both more numerous
and more pointed.[14] This is hardly surprising. The 'Dream of

---

[12] Block (1980) notes the thematic significance of Virgil's emphasis on the
slaughter of the young and the way in which this is highlighted through a
series of intertextual relationships with the *Iliad*; it is, however, the
relationship with the myth of Er that allows us to lay moral responsibility for
this slaughter directly on Aeneas' choice of a life.

[13] Cf. Boyle (1986), 154-56.

[14] On the links between the 'Dream of Scipio' and *Aeneid* 6 see Hardie (1986),
71-76, though Hardie tends to talk in terms of 'influence' rather than
'intertextuality'. Similarly Camps (1969), 89f., speaks of 'reminiscence' and
'inherited materials' without addressing the functional nature of Virgil's

Scipio' constitutes the mythic closure of Cicero's *De Re Publica*, a work in which Cicero articulates the ideology of the Roman state; as the author has his protagonist Scipio say, this is not a description of some fictitious ideal society in the manner of Plato but a historical account of the development of the Roman republic to its mature and healthy condition, its *optimus status* (*DRP* 2.16.30). The virtue that it extols is that of civic duty, of service to the state, as the authorial introduction to Book 1 makes clear:

> neque enim est ulla res, in qua propius ad deorum numen uirtus accedat humana, quam ciuitatis aut condere nouas aut conseruare iam conditas.
>
> (*DRP* 1.7.12)

> For there is no other area in which human virtue more closely approaches the divinity of the gods than in the founding of new states or the preservation of those already founded.

Contemplation of the past is to provide a moral paradigm for present action, particularly with regard to those who occupied the position of 'first man in Rome', the *rector/moderator/princeps/ summus uir rei publicae*.[15] So too for Anchises the parade of Roman heroes provides incitement to action:

---

divergence. Cf. also Habinek (1989), who deals at length with the *DRP* (234f., 248-51) but likewise fails to appreciate how the intertextuality affects our response to the *content* of Virgil's text. See also Klingner (1967), 491f.; Feeney (1986), 1f.

[15] On this figure and the ideology underpinning Cicero's *DRP* generally, see Penwill (1994), 70-76.

et dubitamus adhuc uirtutem extendere factis,
aut metus Ausonia prohibet consistere terra?

(Aeneid 6.807f.)

And do we still hesitate to expand our virtue by deeds, or
does fear inhibit us from establishing ourselves on Auso-
nian soil?

What for Cicero are the *imagines* of notable historical figures and
the *optimus status* of the republic are for Anchises the souls of
those about to play their part in the establishment of the Roman
state and Roman world-domination; in terms of their espousal of
civic virtue, their ideological positions are indistinguishable.

In the 'Dream of Scipio' as in *Aeneid* 6 the ideology is given a
cosmic reference, and Virgil carefully sets up the parallels in his
narration. The dream aspect is evoked by the appearance of
Anchises to Aeneas at 5.726ff., by the comparison of Anchises'
imago to a 'fleeting dream' at 6.702 (itself an echo of a twice-used
simile from *Odyssey* 11: 11.207 and 222), and by the Gates of
Sleep of 6.893ff. (of which—naturally—more later). The other-
worldly encounter between son and father recalls that between
grandson and grandfather in the earlier work (the relationship in
the *Aeneid* being emphasised by the formulaic repetition of *pater
Anchises* ['father Anchises'] at the same position in the line at
6.679, 713, 854, 867); and in both cases the *imago* of the departed
ancestor uses the opportunity to engage in prophecy, encourage-
ment and cosmic revelation, and to answer questions. The parallelism extends even to details of cosmology: both Anchises and the
elder Scipio represent the stars and planets as animated by divine
mind (*SS* 15; *Aen.* 6.724-27) and fire as the element that predo-

minates in the soul (*SS* 15; *Aen.* 6.730f.). And in both cases it is the happy place, the Elysian Fields in the *Aeneid* or a fixed habitation in heaven in the 'Dream of Scipio', that is both the dwelling-place of the souls of the virtuous after death and the source of souls destined to play a major role on the Roman political stage in the future. So the elder Africanus:

> sed quo sis, Africane, alacrior ad tutandam rem publicam, sic habeto: omnibus, qui patriam conseruauerint, adiuuerint, auxerint, certum esse in caelo definitum locum, uti beati aeuo sempiterno fruantur; nihil est enim illi principi deo, qui omnem mundum regit, quod quidem in terris fiat, acceptius quam concilia coetusque hominum iure sociati, quae ciuitates appellantur; harum rectores et conseruatores hinc profecti huc reuertuntur.
>
> (*SS* 13 = *DRP* 6.13.13)

> But, Africanus, so that you may be the more eager to guard the *res publica*, carry this thought with you: that for all those who have saved, aided, expanded their fatherland there is an assigned place in heaven, where in blessedness they enjoy eternal life; for as far as what happens on earth is concerned, nothing is more acceptable to that *princeps* god who regulates the universe than the assemblies and gatherings of men bound together by justice which are called states; their regulators and preservers come from and return to this place.

And impressed (as who could not be) by the fact that the extra-corporeal existence of these souls is far superior to that of souls imprisoned in bodies, that it is in fact true life as opposed to the 'death' that is life on earth, the younger Scipio asks the soul of his natural father Aemilius Paulus the obvious question:

> quaeso, inquam, pater sanctissime atque optime, quoniam
> haec est uita, ut Africanum audio dicere, quid moror in
> terris? quin huc ad uos uenire propero?
>
> > (*SS* 15 = *DRP* 6.15.15)

> 'I ask you,' I said, 'most holy and best of fathers, since this
> is life, as I hear Africanus say, why do I hang around on
> earth? Why not hasten here to you?'

Aeneas, on being told that the horde of souls he sees congregating on the banks of Lethe are destined for reincarnation, makes a similar enquiry of Anchises:

> o pater, anne aliquas ad caelum hinc ire putandumst
> sublimis animas iterumque ad tarda reuerti
> corpora? quae lucis miseris tam dira cupido?[16]
>
> > (*Aeneid* 6.719-21)

> O father, must we suppose that souls journey upwards from
> here to the sky above and once more return into sluggish
> bodies? What perverse desire for light afflicts the poor
> things?

---

[16] A good discussion of the significance of this question to Aeneas may be found in Di Cesare (1974), 114f. Bishop's (1988) dismissal of it as being about no more than 'the mechanics of rebirth' (125) is clearly unjustifiable.

Paulus responds to Scipio's query with a thoroughly Roman reply: God has stationed us here on earth and we must remain at our post until he chooses to issue a recall; your task is to follow the example of your ancestors (*mos maiorum* again), cultivate *iustitia* and *pietas*, deserve well of the republic and you'll be here with us in the fullness of time. Obviously a similar *pietas*-based answer is available to Anchises, but he does not give it; instead, he embarks on the rambling and confused cosmology of 724ff.[17] which has none of the moral conviction of either Plato or Cicero[18] and in the end does not answer the question at all.[19] All he can offer by way of explanation is that these souls have drunk a sufficient quantity of the waters of Lethe to forget the fact that death is better than life—or that life in the pastoral pleasance of Elysium is absolutely

---

[17] So Farrell (1991), 87: 'Anchises' description...presents the reader with an almost unintelligibly confused and eclectic eschatology.' The confusion is deliberate, and simply to say that it is a consequence of Virgil's drawing on a multiplicity of sources (as for example Horsfall [1981], 145) is not a sufficient explanation.

[18] The synthetic nature of Anchises' discourse is noted by Gransden (1990), 83, but he like many other commentators persists in seeing this speech as profound and revelatory. Cf. in particular Austin (1977), 220-21, who claims that it manifests 'such visionary beauty and earnest solemnity [that] it is as if the poet were "thinking aloud", giving expression to his most inmost beliefs.' It is unfortunate that so many neglect to observe the quotation marks that surround this and the other major ideological statements in the poem.

[19] Otis (1964) rightly points out that 'the question is crucial', that 'any attempt to find consistency' in Anchises' response 'is futile', and that 'the "answer" is in one sense disappointing'. Otis' use of quotation marks around 'answer' is revealing (it is not a real *answer*, only a reply); his 'in one sense' is puzzling, since there seems no sense in which this 'answer' is *not* 'disappointing'. Di Cesare's (1974) claim (116) that 'the discourse answers Aeneas' question by denying its terms' recognises the disjunction between question and answer but obscures the obvious conclusion to be drawn from it. Di Cesare's discussion here as elsewhere is flawed by ignoring the intertextual references; while I have considerable sympathy for his eschewing what he flatteringly calls 'the venerable art of *Quellenforschung*' (preface viii), one simply cannot read the *Aeneid* without being alive to the way in which Virgil generates meaning through allusion.

preferable to the rat-race of Roman politics. In Plato's 'Myth of Er' the souls after choosing their lives journey across a waterless desert and drink because they are thirsty; forgetfulness comes as a by-product of their drinking. In the *Aeneid* forgetfulness is the primary purpose, to wipe out all consciousness of what espousal of the imperial ideology entails, of what it requires one to abandon. And we might note here another important divergence from the Ciceronian account. For Cicero the reward of virtue is a place in heaven (whether one regards this literally or as an allegory of individual happiness, the 'warm inner glow' which comes with consciousness of having done the right thing); earthly fame is at best a worthless incidental, as the elder Africanus expounds at length (*SS* 17-23). Anchises has no such heavenly reward to offer: instead of the cosmic vision offered by the elder Africanus to his grandson as the ultimate recompense for the pursuit of civic virtue, the reward offered to Aeneas is that his actions will ultimately lead to the establishment of the golden age by Augustus (*Aen.* 6.791ff.). And at the end, all he has to inspire his son is the promise of earthly fame: *incenditque animum famae uenientis amore*, 'he inflames his son with love of fame to come' (6.889).[20] The shade of Palinurus, who stuck to his post until it killed him, testifies to the hollow nature of this reward.[21]

---

[20] Feeney (1986), 4, notes the discrepancy between Anchises' position and Scipio's—although he expresses it as that between 'Vergil's' and 'Cicero's'. But Feeney well brings out the way in which Virgil's casting of Anchises' speech makes it anything but the unqualified panegyric on 'the grandeur that will be Rome' that its deliverer thinks he has produced (*ibid.* 6-16).

[21] Cf. Segal (1966a), 45-49. Segal notes the echo in Aeneas' question of the sibyl's *unde haec, o Palinure, tibi tam dira cupido* ('Whence comes this perverse desire of yours, Palinurus?', 6.373): not only does this make us think of Palinurus here, but also it suggests that to Aeneas the desire of souls to be reborn is as contrary to the established order of things as Palinurus' desire to enter the realm of the dead before receiving the proper funeral rites.

One other point about Aeneas' question, and one which further prepares us for the ending of the book, is its Lucretian quality. Both verbally and thematically it echoes Lucretius' poem: verbally in its positioning of *putandumst* ('must it be thought?') at the end of the line (only here in the *Aeneid*, 23 times in the *De Rerum Natura*, thus giving it the quality of a Lucretian formula) and in the similar placing of *cupido* ('lust') in line 721; thematically in its evocation of the arguments against the lust for life in the last section of Book 3:

> denique tanto opere in dubiis trepidare periclis
> quae mala nos subigit uitai tanta cupido?
>
> (*DRN* 3.1076f.)

> Finally what evil and vast desire for life compels us to endure this level of anxiety in the midst of dangers whose outcome we cannot predict?

The allusion serves to remind us of the fact that the notion of souls queuing up to be born is one that is specifically derided at *DRN* 3.776-83. There are also important echoes of the Lucretian style in Anchises' speech as he moves into didactic mode: *principio* ('first', 774), *quin et* ('yes, not even', 735), *necessest* ('it must be that', 737), *scilicet* ('so that, you see', 750), *nunc age* ('come now', 756), *expediam dictis* ('I shall set forth in words', 759), *lumina uitae* ('light of life', 828).[22] The irony of the way in which Anchises is made to echo Lucretius even as he attempts to invest his material with a completely opposite colouring is telling and

---

[22] With the exception of the last two cases, I give Day Lewis's (1966) translation of these expressions.

significant.[23] The *fasces...saeuasque securis* ('rods and cruel axes')
won by Brutus at *Aen.* 6.818f. cannot fail to call to mind Lucretius'
use of the same formula at *DRN* 3.995f. as he produces Sisyphus
as paradigm of the futility of pursuing political power;[24] Anchises'
laudumque immensa cupido ('immense lust for praises') at *Aen.*
6.823[25] recalls Lucretius' *honorum caeca cupido* ('blind lust for
honours') at *DRN* 3.59; and right at the centre of the great ideological passage (*Aen.* 6.847-53) the phrase *regere imperio* ('rule by
your command', 851) catches Lucretius' *ut satius multo iam sit
parere quietum/quam regere imperio res uelle et regna tenere* ('so
it is much better to obey in peace than to wish to rule the world by
your command and possess kingdoms', *DRN* 5. 1129f.)[26] Even as
Anchises most passionately pleads his case for the moral

---

[23] The Lucretian echoes are noted by Michels (1944), 147, and Habinek (1989),
240. Michels notes the diametrically opposite nature of Anchises discourse
('That a doctrine so utterly opposed to his own should be presented in such a
way that one could almost swear the words were spoken by Lucretius
himself...would be enough to make even his ashes spin in their urn') but
draws no conclusion from it; for Habinek, the issue is one of style rather than
content. The point is also observed by Gransden (1990), 82f., and by Powell,
(1992), 143. Powell sees in these echoes a 'rebuke' delivered by Virgil to his
predecessor, a deliberate evocation of Lucretian language to deliver a
diametrically opposite message. But Virgil's normal practice in creating
intertextual reference is to endow his text with greater subtlety rather than
engage in polemic (*pace* Thomas [1986], 185-88); and in a context in which a
major question mark is about to be placed against Anchises' representation of
events both cosmological and political, I think it is clear that we are dealing
with irony, not rebuke.

[24] *Sisyphus...qui petere a populo fasces saeuasque securis/imbibit* ('Sisyphus
...who thirsts to seek from the people the rods and cruel axes').

[25] It is by no means irrelevant to note that this—coupled with *amor patriae*,
'love of the fatherland' (here overshadowing the love that is due to one's
children)—is precisely what impels Brutus to kill his sons: cf. Block (1980),
136.

[26] Cf. Lyne (1994), 193f. Michels (1944), 148, sees this as Virgil 'challenging'
Lucretius by using the echo to emphasise his divergence from the Epicurean
doctrine of non-participation in public affairs. The same argument applies
against this position as against that of Powell: see n.23 above.

justification of empire, these Lucretian echoes keep intruding to undercut and negate the position he is advocating.

And so we come to the gate of false dreams. It is strange that the obvious meaning of the closing lines of *Aeneid* 6 has still not been universally accepted. If the ivory gate is that through which the *manes* ('spirits of the dead') send *falsa insomnia* ('false dreams') to the world above, then to have Anchises, one of the *manes*, send Aeneas and the Sibyl through that gate is to identify them as false dreams; that is, like the dream despatched by Zeus to Agamemnon in *Iliad* 2, they are bearers of false information. To try to escape this conclusion is to engage in linguistic contortion. Take Gordon Williams for example:[27]

> It is suggested that our knowledge of what happened to Aeneas in the underworld is analogous to a deceptive dream. This does not mean that what is known is untrue, but that it needs interpretation.

Falsa I would suggest does not mean 'requiring interpretation', but 'false'. Nor is it an argument to say that Virgil has no choice but to have Anchises send Aeneas and the sibyl through the ivory gate because the gate of horn is reserved for *ueris umbris* ('true shades', 894), and that therefore the fact that they leave this way has limited or no significance.[28] As comparison with the *Odyssey* passage to which he is alluding shows (19.562-67),[29] Virgil has

---

[27] Williams (1983), 57.
[28] See e.g. Williams (1985), 77; Austin (1977), 276; Reed (1973), 311-15.
[29] For detailed comparison of *Aeneid* 6.893-96 and *Odyssey* 19.562-67 plus discussion of the significance of the gate of false dreams in the *Aeneid*, see Boyle (1986), 142-46. Boyle's is by far the most lucid and logical exposition of a passage on which commentators have shown a peculiar willingness to

deliberately rewritten it to make it impossible for Aeneas to leave by the gate of horn: that is, he has chosen to deny himself that option.[30] *That* is what 'needs interpretation'. To have Aeneas and the sibyl despatched by the ivory gate brands everything with which they have been invested as a false or deceptive dream—the moral justification of empire which constitutes the climax of Anchises' prophetic speech (6.847-53), the ideology of the golden age, the idea that playing the role of statesman is a virtuous activity, the value of fame, the whole notion that the universe is governed by a rational principle which ensures that the good are rewarded and the evil punished: all these and more are thus called into question. Like the οὖλος Ὄνειρος ('evil Dream') sent by Zeus to Agamemnon at *Iliad* 2.5ff., Anchises instils in Aeneas and the Sibyl a false hope; and as Homer's Dream adopts the likeness of the venerable figure of Nestor to give its deceptive message an aura of verisimilitude, so in Virgil empire's specious ideology is put into the mouth of *pater Anchises*, whose words *pius Aeneas* is bound to respect.[31] But the fact that the gate of ivory is Aeneas' and the Sibyl's only means of egress adds another dimension. The implication here is that anyone who uses the dead as a source of moral instruction for the living, who looks in the past to find a

---

engage in all kinds of prevarications to avoid drawing the obvious conclusion. See in particular West (1987), who follows the familiar pattern of subjecting previous interpretations to withering criticism as a prelude to producing an even more abstruse one of his own.

[30] I cannot therefore agree with the conclusion of Brenk (1992), 282, that 'reference to the *Odyssey* passage is a clear solution only to the distinction between the Gates, not to the reason for Aeneas' exit from the Porta Eburna'. The intertextual relationship is much more profound.

[31] This would not be the first time that Anchises has misled Aeneas; see esp. 3.102ff. Powell (1992), 146, observes the 'grave imperfections' with which Virgil has endowed Aeneas' father, but fails to apply this observation to the role assigned to him in Book 6.

moral paradigm for the present, who seeks, as we might say, an ethical imperative from the other side, is necessarily and inevitably deluding both himself and his fellow human beings. In its way this is as emphatic an attack on the traditional Roman aristocratic value system, the *mos maiorum*, as that of Lucretius a generation earlier;[32] it also represents this poet's judgment on the policy of a government and a *princeps* whose ideology and rhetoric was so firmly based on the values of the past. If we have been reading *Aeneid* 6 with a proper appreciation of its intertextual allusions, the fact that it ends as it does should cause us little surprise.

---

[32] For an analysis of this aspect of Lucretius' *De Rerum Natura*, see esp. Minyard (1985), 33-70.

CHAPTER 2

THE FABLE OF THE BEES

Images of the City in *Georgics* 4

> So work the honey-bees,
> Creatures that by a rule in Nature teach
> The Act of Order to a peopled kingdom.
> (Shakespeare, *Henry V*, 1.2.187-89)

IN the programmatic statement at the opening of *Georgics* 4, the 'book of bees', Virgil employs language which clearly indicates that an analogy is to be drawn between the bee community and human society:[1]

> magnanimosque duces totiusque ordine gentis
> mores et studia et populos et proelia dicam.
>
> *(Georgics* 1.4f.)
>
> And I shall tell you of great-hearted leaders and of the customs, interests, communities and battles of an entire nation.

In drawing this analogy, Virgil is following good epic and philosophical precedent. Both Homer and Hesiod analogise from

---

[1] That Virgil's bee community functions as an image of a human one is widely acknowledged. See e.g. Dahlmann (1954) *passim*; Otis (1964), 181; Joudoux (1971), 67; Perkell (1978), 212; Connor (1979), 41; Putnam (1979), 250; Miles (1980), 226f.; Farrell (1991), 239.

bee to human: Homer in the first extended or 'epic' simile of the *Iliad* (2.87-93), where the assembling of the Achaian warriors is compared to the massing of swarms of bees in springtime,[2] and Hesiod in the *Theogony* version of the Pandora story (*Th.* 594-602), where women are compared to drones who live off the labour of bees in the hive. On the philosophic side we find Plato also using the drone analogy in his account of the transition from oligarchy through democracy to tyranny at *Politeia* 552c ff., and there are a couple of other analogic references to the social and swarming habits of bees in the *Phaedo* (82b) and the *Politicus* (293d). Virgil's own use of the analogy in the celebrated bee simile to describe the building activity of the Carthaginians at *Aeneid* 1.430-36 furnishes yet another example; the fact that this simile consists almost entirely of phrases and lines recycled from *Georgics* 4.162-69 merely serves as another indication of how readily the *Georgics*' account of the bees can be read as a model of human social order.[3]

Thus far there is little controversy. The question really is the extent to which this description has a specifically Roman reference; there is no difficulty about saying that Virgil's beehive represents or is analogous to *a* city (the *Aeneid* passage shows this well enough), but what about *the* city? In this chapter I will attempt to answer this question by looking at particular characteristics of the bee community and examining the intertextual

---

[2] The fact that this is the *Iliad*'s first extended simile is observed by Farrell (1991), 252; the significance of Virgil's use of it is discussed below, pp.54-56.

[3] For a detailed analysis of the way in which *Georgics* narrative is appropriated in this and the other bee-similes of the *Aeneid*, see Leach (1977) and Briggs (1980), 68-81.

relationships that Virgil sets up with earlier texts, notably Cicero's *De Re Publica*.

At 4.149ff., Virgil outlines the nature bestowed upon the bees by Jupiter:

> solae communis natos, consortia tecta
> urbis habent, magnisque agitant sub legibus aeuum,
> et patriam solae et certos nouere penatis;
> uenturaeque hiemis memores aestate laborem
> experiuntur et in medium quaesita reponunt.
>
> > (*Georgics* 4.153-57)

> Alone they hold their offspring in common, alone they hold the buildings of their city in common; they pass their life under great laws; alone they know what it is to have a fatherland and acknowledged household gods; and mindful of the coming winter they set themselves to work in summer, putting everything they gather into a common store.

It is here that the human characteristics of the bees are brought out very clearly. Their ability to engage in co-operative activity and their sense of shared ownership is one. Normally this is seen as an allusion to the life prescribed for the Guardians in Plato's *Politeia* which both forbids private property 'apart from the barest essentials' (416d ff.) and requires that 'all the women should be common to all the men; similarly children should be held in common, and no parent should know its child or child its parent' (457c ff.).[4] But I do not think we should leave it at that. To take private property first: while no Roman aristocrat would go so far

---

[4] So e.g. Conington (1865), *ad* 4.153, citing Servius.

as to argue against this concept altogether, the notion of shared ownership and purpose is very strong in Roman political philosophy and is in fact enshrined in the very concept of *res publica*. So Scipio argues in Cicero's *De Re Publica*:

> est igitur res publica res populi, populus autem non omnis hominum coetus quoque modo congregatus, sed coetus multitudinis iuris consensu et utilitatis communione sociatus.
>
> (*DRP* 1.25.39)

> So a *res publica* is the property of a people; a 'people', though, is not every congregation of human beings brought together in any kind of way, but one of a large number of individuals associated in a common sense of what is right and a partnership for the common benefit.

The sense of commonality is as strong in Scipio's *consensu* and *communione* as in Virgil's *communis* and *consortia*; and we should not forget that the idea of 'public property' is much nearer the surface of the phrase *res publica* than it is in the English derivative.[5] One might consider also Cicero's words in the *De Officiis*, where, talking about the grades of *societates hominum*, Cicero says of shared *ciuitas*:

> multa enim sunt ciuibus inter se communia, forum, fana, porticus, uiae, leges, iura, iudicia, suffragia, consuetudines praeterea et familiaritates multisque cum multis res rationesque contractae.
>
> (*De Off.* 1.17.53)

---

5 See Wood (1988), 125f.; Zetzel (1995), 127f.

> For fellow-citizens have many things in common: forum,
> temples, colonnades, streets, laws, principles of justice,
> courts, voting systems, social contacts what's more and
> groups of friends plus many business and commercial
> transactions with a multitude of people.

The *consortia tecta* ('common buildings') of the bees have their
counterparts in the Roman *urbs* in public buildings in which
transactions pertaining to the common good are undertaken.
Virgil's bee community is much closer to this conception of
communal ownership than Plato's Guardians, who constitute only
one class in a wider social structure. Private property in Plato is
certainly not forbidden to the artisans; participation in government,
what a Roman would call *res publica*, certainly is.

The idea of *communes nati*, 'offspring in common', is not
merely Platonist fancy, either. It is linked to the concept of *patria*,
'fatherland', which is specifically ascribed to the bees at 4.155,
and which is of course an integral part of the Roman *Weltan-
schauung*. In the Roman community, children are certainly
recognised as 'belonging' to particular families (the Roman system
of naming lays much more emphasis on this than the Greek), but at
the same time they are all in an important sense the 'children' of
the fatherland, with all the obligations that entails. This sense of
double parentage is brought out in Cicero's *Laws*, where the idea is
canvassed that Roman citizens born outside Rome have in fact two
fatherlands, one by birth (*ortu*) and one by citizenship (*ciuitate*);
and it is emphatically stated that it is the latter which has the
paramount claim on filial duty:

> sed necesse est caritate eam [*sc* patriam] praestare, qua rei
> publicae nomen uniuersae ciuitatis est; pro qua mori et cui
> nos totos dedere et in qua nostra omnia ponere et quasi
> consecrare debemus. dulcis autem non multo secus est ea,
> quae genuit, quam illa, quae excepit.
>
> (*Laws* 2.2.5)

> But it is necessary that that [fatherland] should stand first in
> our affection in which the name of *res publica* is that of
> common citizenship; for that one we are obliged to die, to
> that one we are obliged to hand ourselves over entirely, on
> that one we are obliged to place and as it were consecrate
> all our possessions. And yet the one which gave us birth is
> not much less sweet than the one which took us over.

Thus as far as Rome is concerned, she receives us as *communis
natos*, and the *pietas* which defines our moral duty to her differs in
degree, not kind, from that which defines our duty to our natural
parents.

The more obviously Roman aspects of Virgil's bee-description
here (apart from *patria*) are the *magnae leges* of 4.154 and the
certi penates of 4.155. The idea of a community 'living under
great laws' and the recognition that this is part of *natura*
(remember that this is part of a list of attributes outlining the
natura which Jupiter has granted to the bees) is totally within the
spirit of Cicero's political philosophy as articulated in the *Laws*
and elsewhere: see e.g. *Laws* 1.6.18, *lex est ratio summa insita in
natura, quae iubet ea, quae facienda sunt, prohibetque contraria*,
'law is the supreme reason implanted in nature, which prescribes
what ought to be done and prohibits the opposite.' *Penates* is an
archetypically Roman concept, and placed here reinforces the aura
of Romanness already established by *larem* at 4.43. Cecropian
bees these may be (177), but the Attic honey they manufacture has

a distinctly Roman flavour; so too the political ideas we have been discussing may have their origin in the Academy and the Stoa, but refracted through the work of Cicero have now become part of the Roman way of thinking about the nature of society. The next generation of bees is no longer Cecropian but *Quirites* (201).[6]

At 4.158ff. Virgil goes into more details about the bees' lifestyle, in which the emphasis is heavily placed on the division of labour: *aliae* (158), *pars* (159), *aliae* (162), *aliae* (163), *sunt quibus* (165), an emphasis extended further in the distinction between the tasks allotted to the *grandaeui* and the *minores* (178-83) as the description resumes after the Cyclops simile. Here again we are invited to think of Plato and the principle of justice enunciated by Socrates in his *Politeia*: τὰ ἑαυτοῦ πράττειν, 'doing one's own task' (433a ff.). But once again it is Cicero rather than Plato to whom Virgil is principally alluding. The overriding notion is that of unity in diversity, as the different tasks allotted to particular groups or classes meld together in a harmonious and integrated whole: *feruet opus, redolentque thymo fragrantia mella* ('the work seethes, and the honey reeks fragrant with thyme', 4.169); *omnibus una quies operum, labor omnibus unus* ('for all there is one rest from toil, for all the work is one', 4.184). This notion of unity in diversity is the hallmark of Scipio's mixed constitution, the only one in which the Ciceronian ideal of a *concordia ordinum* could flourish. Scipio himself draws the analogy between harmony in the state and musical harmony:

---

[6] The specifically Roman nature of the beehive is summarised by Briggs (1980), 69, who remarks that 'the hive is described in terms of a Roman house'. More generally on the Romanness of the bees see Griffin (1979), 95f.; Johnson (1984), 16f.

ut enim in fidibus aut tibiis atque ut in cantu ipso ac
uocibus concentus est quidam tenendus ex distinctis sonis,
quem immutatum aut discrepantem aures eruditae ferre non
possunt, isque concentus ex dissimillimarum uocum
moderatione concors tamen efficitur et congruens, sic ex
summis et infimis et mediis interiectis ordinibus ut sonis
moderata ratione ciuitas consensu dissimillimorum concinit; et quae harmonia a musicis dicitur in cantu, ea est in
ciuitati concordia, artissimum atque optimum omni in re
publica uinculum incolumitatis, eaque sine iustitia nullo
pacto esse potest.

(DRP 2.42.69)

For as in the case of lyres and flutes and of the actual
voices of singers a certain harmony must be maintained
composed out of distinct sounds, change and discord in
which the trained ear cannot abide, and as that harmony
through the management of a set of thoroughly unlike notes
is rendered nonetheless concordant and properly blended,
so does a state sing harmoniously through the agreement of
thoroughly unlike elements, effected by rational management in the intermingling of the highest, lowest and middle
orders as if they were sounds. What is termed 'harmony' by
musicians in singing is *concordia* in the state, the strongest
and best binding to prevent damage in every *res publica*,
and this *concordia* cannot in any way exist without justice.

The 'unity in diversity' aspect is brought out very strongly in this
passage by the striking interspersal of *con-* and *dis-* compounds:
*concentus, distinctis, discrepantem, concentus, dissimillimarum,
concors, congruens, consensu dissimillimorum, concinit, concordia*. The impossibility of *concordia* without *iustitia* is acknowledged in the bee community through the *magnae leges* according
to which they live their lives (4.154). The musical harmony of the

well-orchestrated state is echoed in the contented humming of the bees at 4..188—a sound be it noted quite other than that which emanates from the hive of sick bees at 4.260-63 by which the trained ear of the beekeeper can tell that something is badly wrong, or from the bees in the grip of *discordia* at 4.67ff. (note esp. *Martius ille aeris rauci canor increpat, et uox/auditur fractos sonitus imitata tubarum,* 'that martial tone of raucous bronze clashes out, and a sound is heard imitating the fractured notes of the trumpet', 71f.).[7]

The musical analogy has of course its precedent in Plato's *Politeia* (see e.g. 443d, where the just man is said to keep the three elements of his soul in tune like the various notes on a scale). But the Ciceronian use of this image plays not on the tuning of a single instrument but on the proper control of a diverse musical ensemble. Further, the interaction of *con-* and *dis-* compounds in the passage from the end of *De Re Publica* 2 to which I have just referred not only emphasises the way in which disparate elements within the *res publica* act in concert but also draws attention to the essentially Heraclitean nature of human societies: the ἁρμονία within them is like that of Heraclitus' lyre, παλίντονος ('back-stretched'), a tension between opposing forces, and thus they contain within themselves the seeds of their own dissolution. That this is inherent in the nature of things is suggested by Scipio

---

7 Farrell (1991) notes that the tripartite simile of *Georgics* 4.261-63 comparing the sound of sick bees to that of wind, sea and fire echoes Homer's tripartite simile (sea, fire, wind) illustrating the warcries of Achaians and Trojans δεινὸν ἀϋσσάντων at *Iliad* 14.392-401 (cf. also Putnam [1979], 268f.). The Homeric allusion strengthens the thematic link between *discordia* and sickness established in general terms by comparison with violent and raucous (elemental/unbridled) sounds. On the structural level this link has already been established by the parallel Lucretian (in the sense of violent and abrupt) endings of Books 1 and 3—Book 1 ending with *discordia* and *Mars impius* and Book 3 with the plague.

himself when discussing the secession of the plebs that took place
around 494 BCE:

> sed id, quod fieri natura rerum ipsa cogebat, ut plusculum
> sibi iuris populus adscisceret liberatus a regibus...
> consecutum est; in quo defuit fortasse ratio, sed tamen
> uincit ipsa rerum publicarum natura saepe rationem.
>
> (*DRP* 2.33.57)

> But there followed an event which the very nature of things
> compelled to happen, that the people, freed from their
> kings, claimed for themselves an excessive measure of
> rights...In this perhaps reason was lacking, but the very
> nature of *res publicae* often defeats reason.

The task of keeping the *res publica* together, to maintain that *ratio*
by which and in which harmony resides, belongs to the statesman—or, to pursue the musical analogy a little further, the orch-
estra requires a conductor, a *moderator* as Cicero terms him at
5.6.8 and elsewhere.

The situation in the bee community is very similar:

> rege incolumi mens omnibus una est;
> amisso rupere fidem, constructaque mella
> diripuere ipsae et cratis soluere fauorum.
>
> (*Georgics* 4.212-14)

> While the king is safe they are all of one mind; but if he has
> been lost, they have broken faith, plundered the built-up
> stocks of honey and unravelled the wickerwork of the
> combs.

Here too we find the polarity between *con-* and *dis-* (*constructa/ diripuere*) as the kingless bees tear apart the fruits of their co-operative labour, and we realise that the *innatus amor habendi* ('innate love of possession') that is part of the character that Jupiter has bestowed upon the bees can lead just as easily to selfish plundering as to acquiring honey for the common store: in the absence of their king they behave like the secessionist plebs of the Roman *res publica*.[8] They are after all creatures of the iron age, when all is said and done;[9] and as Plato pointed out their virtue is due to habit, not philosophy (*Phaedo* 82b). Both communities need

---

[8]   The deleterious and divisive effect of *amor habendi* on the Roman *res publica* had become a literary commonplace: see e.g. Lucilius 1145-51 W., Lucretius *DRN* 2.1-54 and the prefaces to Sallust's *War with Catiline* and *War with Jugurtha*. Virgil had already drawn attention to it at *Georgics* 2.495ff. In the bees it is *innatus*, part of their essential nature; thus it cannot be corrected, only regulated.

[9]   They, like the Cyclopes with whom they are associated by way of simile at 4.170-75, are agents of Jupiter; the Cyclopes manufacture the thunderbolts by which Jupiter maintains control, while the bees nourished Jupiter as a baby. Jupiter is the god of the iron age as the theodicy in Book 1 makes clear (1.121-46), and it is expressly stated that the bees' characteristics are dispensed by him (*nunc age, naturas apibus quas Iuppiter ipse/addidit expediam*, 'Come now, and I'll explain the natures that Jupiter himself bestowed upon the bees', 4.149f.). As one might expect, these characteristics are archetypically of the iron age: acquisitiveness (see previous note), militarism, and above all a dedication to *labor*, which shows that they operate fully under Jupiter's dictum *labor omnia uincit* (1.145). See Stehle (1974), 359: 'The bees...represent one attempt to escape destruction by complete adherence to the style of Jupiter's world'; Putnam (1979), 254: 'The bees' existence is a decline from, rather than a reversion to the golden age.' Cf. also Putnam's discussion of the association between the bees and the Cyclopes, *ibid.* 256-59. The contention of Johnston (1980), 90-96, that they retain a number of golden age characteristics (likewise Miles [1980], 245) and thus 'function as a bridge between the metallic golden age and agriculture' seems to me a misreading of their thematic role. They may have access to the honey that man had in the age of Saturn but lost with the advent of Jupiter (cf. 1.131), but their treatment of it is exploitative and acquisitive; and the 'golden' aspect of the honey and their bodies is subverted towards the pursuit of *gloria*: see esp. the appearance of the 'better' king at 4.91.

the controlling hand of a powerful leader: as the bees need their king, so the Roman *res publica* requires its *princeps*, to keep the forces of personal aggrandisement that lead to dissolution under control.

In the authorial preface to Book 5 of his *De Re Publica*, the book which dealt in detail with the character and role of the 'first man in Rome' but which is now largely lost, Cicero attributes the parlous state of the *res publica* in his time to the absence of such a *moderator*:

> itaque ante nostram memoriam et mos ipse patrius prae-
> stantes uiros adhibebat, et ueterem morem ac maiorum
> instituta retinebant excellentes uiri....[nunc autem] de uiris
> quid dicam? mores enim ipsi interierunt uirorum penuria,
> cuius tanti mali non modo reddenda ratio nobis, sed etiam
> tamquam reis capitis quodam modo dicenda causa est.
> nostris enim uitiis, non casu aliquo, rem publicam uerbo
> retinemus, re ipsa uero iam pridem amisimus.
>
> (*DRP* 5.1.1-2)

> And so before our time we find both that the customs of our
> forefathers produced pre-eminent men and that outstanding
> men kept in place the ancient customs and institutions of
> our ancestors....[But now] what can I say about the men?
> Our very customs have perished because of the lack of
> men, and for so great a calamity we must not only render
> account but plead our case in whatever way we can as if we
> were facing a capital charge. For it is through our faults, not
> because of some bad luck, that while we preserve a *res
> publica* in word, in reality we have long lost it.

It is the statesman who is finally responsible for the community's material and moral well-being:

> huic moderatori rei publicae beata ciuium uita proposita est,
> ut opibus firma, copiis locuples, gloria ampla, uirtute
> honesta sit.
>
> *(DRP* 5.6.8)*

> This *moderator* of the *res publica* has as his object a happy
> life for the citizens, one which is stable thanks to its wealth,
> rich in resources, great in glory and honoured in virtue.

So with the bees: their wealth they store in their 'treasure-house'
(*thesauri*, 4.253) guarantees the stability of the hive in the winter
months, their resources are the flowers and herbs of summer near
which the beekeeper has placed their hive, their glory is in the
production of honey (cf. *generandi gloria mellis*, 205), and the
'virtue' for which they are honoured is their willingness to
sacrifice their lives not only in pursuit of this glory (203f.) but also
in the defence of their king (*pulchramque petunt per uulnera
mortem*, 'and they seek a noble death through their wounds', 218).
The honour and loyalty they display towards their king is yet
another way in which they live up to Ciceronian principle: 'The
princeps of a state must be nourished by glory, and the *res publica*
will only last as long as the *princeps* is shown honour by all' (*DRP*
5.7.9)[10].

---

[10] The reference to the peoples of the east with which Virgil introduces his
account of the bees' devotion to their king (4.210-12) has led some to suggest
that this is an un-Roman characteristic. Cf. Leach (1977), 5: 'Such simple,
self-sacrificing dedication to a king which exceeds even that of the servile
Lydians and Persians can scarcely be meant as an example for Romans, but
rather suggests the emotional precariousness of citizens and the danger to a
sound state that comes from adherence to a sole ruler.' Similarly Perkell
(1978), 213; Miles (1980), 249f. But the Ciceronian allusion clearly supports
the view expressed above.

THE FABLE OF THE BEES

It is significant I think that immediately after the passage in which Virgil describes the bees' reliance on and loyalty to their king we find the following:

> his quidam signis atque haec exempla secuti
> esse apibus partem diuinae mentis et haustus
> aetherios dixere...
>
> *(Georgics* 4.219-21)

> Because of these signs and following these examples, some have said that bees have a part of the divine mind and partake of ethereal draughts.

In one sense this is merely the logical extension of describing bees in human terms: so like human beings have they become to our imagination that they begin to share that kinship with God that is affirmed by Cicero and others to be that which separates man from the rest of creation (see e.g. *Laws* 1.8.24, 1.22.59). Indeed, as Virgil's following lines (221-24) suggest, the same may be said of all animal creation after we have encountered it in the way Virgil directs us in the second half of his poem. But the fact that this comes immediately after the passsage on kings constitutes a specific reference to Cicero's *De Re Publica*: for in that work the discussion of the role of the *princeps* which clearly occupied Book 5 and the early part of Book 6 is immediately followed by the Dream of Scipio, in which the role of the statesman is given a cosmic reference:

> nihil est enim illi principi deo, qui omnem mundum regit,
> quod quidem in terris fiat, acceptius quam concilia

coetusque hominum iure sociati, quae ciuitates appellantur;
harum rectores et conseruatores hinc profecti huc reuer-
tuntur.

(*DRP* 6.13.13)

For as far as what happens on earth is concerned, nothing is
more acceptable to that *princeps* god who regulates the
universe than the assemblies and gatherings of men bound
together by justice which are called states; their regulators
and preservers come from and return to this place.

The role of god in the universe is analogous to that of the
statesman on earth; indeed, in a very real sense the statesman is
doing god's work as he ensures the smooth running of the
community over which he has charge.[11] As god's regulation of the
universe produces that cosmic harmony which is echoed in the
music of the spheres, so his earthly analogue produces that
harmony of otherwise discordant elements that Scipio described
towards the end of Book 2. For him there is a place reserved in the
heaven from which he came:

ea uita uia est in caelum et in hunc coetum eorum, qui iam
uixerunt et corpore laxati illum incolunt locum, quem
uides...quem uos, ut a Graiis accepistis, orbem lacteum
nuncupatis.

(*DRP* 6.16.16)

That life is the road to heaven and to the company of those
who have lived out their lives and, relieved of their body,
inhabit that place which you see...the place which you,

---

[11] For fuller discussion of this issue see Penwill (1994), 73f.; Luck (1956), 208;
Zetzel (1995), 230f.

taking the term from the Greeks, designate the Milky Circle.

So too with the bees—according to what 'some have said':

> scilicet huc reddi deinde ac resoluta referri
> omnia, nec morti esse locum, sed uiua uolare
> sideris in numerum atque alto succedere caelo.
>
> *(Georgics* 4.225-27)

> Clearly, they say, all things then return hither, dissolved
> and brought back, and there is no place for death: all things
> fly living to the place of a star and climb up to high heaven.

As I argue in the other essay in this book,[12] Virgil sets up a manifest intertextual allusion to Cicero's 'Dream of Scipio' in the last section of *Aeneid* 6; here it seems clear that he is doing the same thing. It is Cicero, I would suggest, who lurks behind the *quidam* ('some') to whom this belief is ascribed at line 219,[13] and

---

12 See above pp.16-22.

13 Commentators dealing with this passage display the same perverse insistence on seeing it as an expression of Virgil's own beliefs as we have already noted with Anchises' speech at *Aeneid* 6.724-51 (cf. above p.21 n.18): so e.g. Williams (1979) *ad loc.*: 'This passage reflects very clearly the pantheistic notion of the *Georgics*, the idea that God is present in every living creature.' Cf. Otis (1964), 186; Mynors (1990), *ad loc.*; Haarhoff (1960), 167f. (this last the most strikingly uncritical). Mynors like many others links this passage with the *Aeneid* one: cf. Klingner (1967), 359-62; Wilkinson (1982), 29; Austin (1977), *ad Aen.* 6.726. Once again the quotation marks—even more manifest here than in the *Aeneid* passage, with *quidam...dixere* plus accusative and infinitive—are either ignored or assigned no significance (Miles [1980], 253, and Thomas [1988] *ad* 4.219-21 are welcome exceptions; Putnam [1979], 264, tries to have it both ways). The danger inherent in such a (non-) critical approach is well put by Thomas (1991), 217: 'Depending on what part of the poem we choose to look at, we could judge [Vergil] (and his whole work, if that is the only part we consider) pantheist, primitivist, atheist or

this whole passage is a fitting climax to a description of a community which manifests so many of the features that Cicero saw as characteristic of Rome at its best.

If this is an *urbs poetica* of the kind I have been arguing for, then an obvious question has to be answered: what is it doing here? The fact that the description gives such prominence to the king, in a way that makes him clearly reflect the Ciceronian *princeps*, makes it very tempting to relate it to the political situation in Italy around the time of Actium. Prior to embarking on his description of the bees' *natura* (on which I have been mainly focusing), Virgil gives an account of battles between rival swarms which he attributes to *discordia* between two kings: *saepe duobus/regibus incessit magno discordia motu*, 67f. Further, the beekeeper is instructed to put the inferior king to death, and given the means to make a simple identification of superior and inferior. It is hard not to see in this a reflection of the rivalry between the two *principes* Octavian and Antony for control of the Roman empire;[14] hard too not to see in the 'easy' identification of the inferior king and his cohorts a comment on the simplistic nature of the propaganda circulating in Rome at the time:[15] we will find Virgil making a

---

animist, Stoic, Democritean, Epicurean, or fundamentalist Olympian, or any combination of these systems and others like them.'

[14] So Nadeau (1984), 77. Miles (1980) agrees that the conflict between the rival swarms is presented as a civil war (*discordia*) and could thus 'have struck a responsive chord in a contemporary Roman audience' (232), but denies any specific reference, arguing that (a) the distinction between the factions is too overdrawn and (b) that in the bees' case the issue is resolved not by themselves but by the beekeeper. Miles's first point is answered in the next note; as far as the second is concerned, I go on to argue that Octavian's role is that of both king bee (politician) and beekeeper (quasi-god).

[15] See for example the contrasting descriptions of the 'careworn' Caesar and the self-indulgent Antony at Plutarch *Antonius* 24, or the nobility and dignity of Octavia as opposed to the shamelessness and *femme fatale* deviousness of Cleopatra, *ibid.* 53f. Plutarch's account throughout shows the influence of

similar comment in his description of the rival forces on Aeneas' shield in *Aeneid* 8. The absolute loyalty demanded of the bees to their king reflects the general necessity for the people to honour their *princeps* as advocated by Cicero; it also I think reflects the particular measures taken by Octavian to secure the loyalty of the Roman people in his war against Antony:[16]

> iurauit in mea uerba tota Italia sponte sua, et me belli quo uici ad Actium ducem depoposcit; iurauerunt in eadem uerba prouinciae Galliae, Hispaniae, Africa, Sicilia, Sardinia.
>
> (*RGDA* 25.2)
>
> The whole of Italy voluntarily swore allegiance to me and demanded me as its leader in the war in which I was victorious at Actium. The provinces of the Gauls, the Spains, Africa, Sicily and Sardinia swore in the same terms.

But the question still remains: if this description reflects contemporary politics, what is Virgil's purpose in making it do so?

There is another player in this game, one we have so far largely been ignoring, and that is the beekeeper. The beekeeper stands very much in the role of god to the bees in his charge;[17] it is he who is responsible for locating the hive in the best possible place, ensuring that it gets neither too hot nor too cold; in this his activity is analogous to that of the gods who establish the temperate zone

---

Octavian's propaganda. For the 'black-and-white' style of propaganda in the years leading up to Actium, see Zanker (1988), 33-77; Syme (1960), 270ff.

[16] Cf. Syme (1960), 284ff.

[17] So Leach (1977), 5: 'One might say that the farmer's arbitration makes his relationship with the bees analogous to the power of the epic gods over men.' Cf. also Johnston (1980), 95.

for human habitation at 1.237ff. It is the beekeeper too who is so easily able to settle the great war between the rival swarms:

> hi motus animorum atque haec certamina tanta
> pulueris exigui iactu compressa quiescent.
> *(Georgics* 4.86f.)

> These high emotions and prodigious contests will be settled
> and made quiet by the throwing of a tiny amount of dust.

What to the bees is a monumental and heroic struggle (reflected in the way their battle is narrated) is to the beekeeper a minor disturbance. The relativity involved reflects again that which we find in Cicero's 'Dream of Scipio', as the elder Africanus demonstrates how poor earthly fame is from the vantage point of heaven (see *DRP* 6.17.17ff.). Furthermore, it is the beekeeper who takes the life of the inferior king in order finally to quell *discordia* in the bee community, intervening to impose his will much as the gods are prone to do in epic poetry from the *Iliad* on. And finally it is for the beekeeper's benefit, not (as they imagine) their own that their perform their allotted tasks—an aspect of their lives that Virgil underscores with the long simile comparing the bees' activity with that of the Cyclopes forging thunderbolts for Jupiter at 4.170-75.

It is here I think that we can discern the point of Virgil's apian *urbs poetica*. Octavian's propaganda cast him in the role of the upholder of traditional Roman values, and he boasts in his memoirs that he held no office that was *contra morem maiorum* ('contrary to the traditions of our ancestors', *RGDA* 6.1). But the supreme power held by him between the expiry of the second triumvirate in 32 BCE and the so-called 'restoration of the republic' in 27 BCE—the period in which the *Georgics* received its final shape and was published—was manifestly unconstitutional, and is glossed over by the words *per consensum uniuersorum potitus rerum omnium* ('having obtained control over everything by universal consent') at *RGDA* 34.1. By presenting the bee community as wholly dependent on a king for the preservation of their prosperity, Virgil hints at the unmentionable reality: a king by any other name....[18] Ciceronian *princeps* undoubtedly was the image Octavian wished to project;[19] Virgil, in setting up his intertextual relationship with Cicero's *De Re Publica*, as so often makes his point by incorporating a crucial divergence: *rex*.[20]

But king bee is not Octavian's only role. While the conclusion to *Georgics* 1 may envision Caesar as the *princeps* whose presence on earth is necessary to restore order to the chaos that has overtaken the human beehive, where work has ceased in favour of war (1.506-08—a situation clearly requiring the supervision of an *operum custos* as the king bee is termed at 4.215) and where

---

[18] The 'king' question had been a significant political issue in Rome in the days of Julius Caesar's dictatorship and Brutus' replay of the expulsion of Tarquinius Superbus. See esp. the graffiti recorded at Suet. *Diu. Iul.* 70.3. There is no reason to suppose that it was no longer an issue in the case of Caesar's heir. Cf. Miles (1980), 249.

[19] Syme (1960), 318-22, denies direct influence of Cicero on Octavian's choice of the role of *princeps*, claiming instead that 'the revolutionary Augustus exploited with art and with success the traditional concepts and the consecrated vocabulary of Roman political literature, much of it, indeed, in no way peculiar to Cicero' (319). But the role ascribed to the *princeps* in the surviving parts of the *DRP* is very like that which the later Augustus was concerned to be seen as fulfilling, and in the years of unconstitutional authority prior to Actium the image of 'leading citizen' would certainly have been regarded as more politically acceptable than that of 'dictator'.

[20] On this link between Virgil's king bee and Roman *rex* (with specific reference to Octavian) cf. Joudoux (1971), 78-81. Oddly Joudoux does not refer at all to the *DRP*.

lawlessness is rampant (note *ruptis legibus* 1.510, echoed in *rupere fidem* 4.213), the prologues to Books 1 and 3 represent him much more as a god, a role in which the *Eclogues*' Tityrus had already cast him.[21] Caesar *diui filius* has his analogue in *Georgics* 4 not just in the king bee but also in the proto-beekeeper Aristaeus, whose father is Apollo Thymbraeus and who 'hopes to attain heaven' (4.325) just as Octavian has all but done.[22] The loss of Aristaeus' bees and their regeneration through the cruel method of *bougonia* is easily seen as an allegory of the destruction of the Roman *res publica* and its alleged regeneration through the bloodshed of proscription and civil war, which reached its tragic climax at the Canopic mouth of the Nile in the summer of 30 BCE (cf. 4.287ff.).[23]

But what has this god achieved? Peace perhaps, but along with peace he brings with him a political program aimed at restoring the values that made Rome great, the *mos maiorum*. Virgil takes significant elements from the work of the political philosopher of the previous generation to offer a kind of *Brave New World* scenario of what such a world would be like.[24] Prosperous and

---

[21] For discussion of the panegyric passages of the *Georgics*, see Boyle (1986), 39-47; on the qualified and ambivalent nature of this panegyric, *ibid.* 76-82, and Nethercut (1973), 43f. and 49f. nn. 5 and 6.

[22] On the parallels between Aristaeus and Octavian, see Boyle (1986), 77 n.90.

[23] Cf. Leach (1977), 3: 'As a legend of rebirth, [*bugonia*] is a final, specific *locus* for a theme that throughout the poem has been pervasively interwoven with the didactic narrative: Vergil's hopes for the regeneration of war-ridden Italy under the new leadership of Octavius Caesar.' Cf. also Miles (1980), 254f. The symbolic nature of *bugonia*, its status as poetic image that is 'unreal but true' is most forcefully argued by Perkell (1989), 75f. and 139ff. On the irony of the Egyptian location, see Nadeau (1984), 72f., and Boyle (1986), 78; there is far more to it than the literary reference to Callimachean aetiology noted by Putnam (1979), 272f.

[24] Kromer (1979), 19, asserts that 'the society of the bees...has often been construed as an image of the ideal Roman state'. Image—caricature?—of a particular idealised construction of the Roman *res publica* perhaps, but hardly

contented it may be, but it is the prosperity and contentment of automatons who have surrendered their individuality to the pursuit of what is represented to them as the common good;[25] and as the comparison with the Cyclopes and the instructions to the beekeeper on how to remove their honey both show, this notion of working for the 'common good', the glory of generating honey, are political fabrications designed to facilitate their exploitation. If Caesar is the beekeeper, then we are working for Caesar, not he for us.

It is in this context that we need to consider the remarkable decision taken by the bees to abjure the joys of Venus:

> illum adeo placuisse apibus mirabere morem
> quod neque concubitu indulgent, nec corpora segnes
> in Venerem soluunt aut fetus nixibus edunt...
>
> (*Georgics* 4.197-99)

You will marvel at the fact that the bees have gone so far as to adopt the following custom, viz. that they neither indulge in bed-sharing nor let themselves become sluggish by relaxing their bodies in sex or bring forth offspring through the pangs of childbirth...

---

ideal. Cf. Otis (1964), 181f.: 'Virgil is...serious in his appreciation of the importance and beneficence of such a purely social or collective existence, but he is serious also in his appreciation of its limitations.'

25 'Automatons', Connor (1979), 43; 'surrendered individuality', Davis (1979), 29. Cf. also Putnam (1979), 11: 'What [the bees] accomplish is by rote. There is no thought in it. They are gifted with nothing parallel to the human imagination. Even their social life demands communistic self-effacement before general public needs.' One is reminded again of Socrates' use of the bee as paradigm of those whose virtue exists by 'habit without philosophy' (Plato *Phaedo* 82b), on which cf. p.15 above.

Commentators have observed that this theory of bee reproduction is known to (but be it noted not accepted by) Aristotle;[26] the issue here, however, is not whether Virgil believed this theory to be correct but the significance of its inclusion in his description of the bee community. For the language used suggests that this is not simply a 'fact of life' or 'law of nature' but something the bees have chosen for themselves: that is surely the import of *placuisse apibus* (lit. '[that this custom] has pleased the bees', 197).[27] Sexual self-indulgence was contrary to the traditional Roman value-system (the story of Lucretia is paradigmatic here), and it was in this regard that Antony was seen by Augustan propaganda as signally deficient;[28] and as with other aspects of Virgil's description of the bees' lifestyle, we see here a particular element of Roman *mos maiorum*—an element that was to find expression in the *lex Iulia de adulteriis coercendis* promulgated by Augustus in 18 BCE—taken to its logical extreme. In Freudian terms, the bees have sublimated their sexual *amor* into the *amor habendi*

---

[26] *HA* 553a.18-26, *GA* 759a.12-14. See Mynors (1990), *ad loc.*

[27] Mynors (1990), *ad* 4.197, interprets *placuisse* to mean that 'they seem contented with it, not resolved on it'. This interpretation ignores the very common impersonal use of *placeo* to denote a course of action resolved upon either formally (as in senatorial or other decrees) or informally (as in a decision made by an individual or group); in either case, it implies conscious decision on the part of the person(s) whom 'it has pleased'. See *OLD* s.v. *placeo* 5.

[28] See e.g. Plutarch *Antonius* 26.1, 52.1, and *Comparison of Demetrius and Antonius* 3.3f. On the general issue see Sallust's portrait of Catiline and his circle (particularly the 'anti-Lucretia' figure of Sempronia, *BC* 25), and compare Scipio's fulminations at the conclusion of Cicero's *DRP* against those who *se corporis uoluptatibus dediderunt earumque se quasi ministros praebuerunt impulsuque libidinum uoluptatibus oboedientium deorum et hominum iura uiolauerunt* ('have given themselves over to the pleasures of the body and made themselves as it were servants of them, and under the impulse of the lusts that minister to these pleasures have violated the laws of gods and men', *DRP* 6.26.29).

('love of possession', 177) discussed above; to an even greater extent than the Guardians of Plato's *Politeia*, they have determined to channel all their energy into working for the common good.[29]

The bees avoid sex because it makes them 'sluggish' (*segnes*, 198);[30] they have in fact chosen to do for themselves what the farmer is instructed to do for the animals in his care in Book 3:

> sed non ulla magis uiris industria firmat
> quam Venerem et caeci stimulos auertere amoris...
>
> (*Georgics* 3.209f.)

> But no kind of attention maintains their strength more than
> averting from them Venus and the goads of blind love.

That *amor* and *labor* are mutually incompatible concepts is one of the overriding themes of the second half of the *Georgics*. It is a theme already adumbrated in the *Eclogues*, particularly in *Eclogue* 10 where the despairing Gallus acknowledges that against this god (Amor) all *labor* is useless (*Ecl.* 10.64); and in the closing stages of the *Georgics,* Orpheus, overcome by the madness of *amor*, looks back at Eurydice and 'all his work is rendered void' (*omnis effusus labor*, 4.491f.). The theme is made more pointed by verbal echoes: *omnia uincit amor* ('love conquers all', *Ecl.* 10.69)~*labor omnia uincit* ('work conquers all', *Georg.* 1.145); *amor omnibus idem* ('love is the same for all', *Georg.* 3.244)~*labor omnibus unus* ('for all the work is one', of the bees at *Georg.* 4.184). But the

---

[29] Cf. Bradley (1968), 348; Miles (1980), 247.

[30] 'The adjective *segnes* is significant: Venus, sexual desire, would make them "sluggish", prevent them from work' (Segal [1966b], 310). The word is applied to the thistle (*carduus*) in the theodicy (1.151f.); *segnitia* in all its manifestations is what the farmer must battle against. Cf. Stehle (1974), 348f.

intertextual allusion goes further than this. The link between the bees' rejection of Venus and the effect of *amor* on animals described at *Georgics* 3.209ff.[31] takes us back to Lucretius' satiric attack on the effects of love on human beings at *DRN* 4.1058ff., where the target is not just Memmius *qua* unenlightened Roman politician but Memmius *qua* love-poet[32]—and not just Memmius, but the whole neoteric movement (Catullus of course in particular) which wallows in the anguish and mental disturbance caused by erotic passion.[33] This confrontation is taken up again in the *Eclogues*, where Gallus the elegiac poet is urged to take up another, didactic,[34] style of poetry in *Eclogue* 6 but is shown in *Eclogue* 10 as unable to do so; he is too much the prisoner of Love and the poetics of Love, as his final words (*omnia uincit amor; et nos cedamus amori*, 'love conquers all; let us too yield to love', 10.69) reveal. *Georgics* 4 is another manifestation of this literary confrontation, where the major players are the bees on the one hand and Orpheus on the other; the bees in their rejection of Venus declare their opposition to the whole ideology of elegiac poetry, where the poet's whole attention is concentrated on *amor* as both love and love-object and grander themes are expressly rejected.[35]

---

[31] Noted by Klingner (1967), 315.

[32] Ovid *Tristia* 2.433.

[33] For fuller discussion of this aspect of *DRN* 4, see Kenney (1970), 380-90 and Minyard (1985), 63-65.

[34] When Gallus is welcomed into the company of Apollo and the Muses at *Eclogue* 6.64ff., Linus presents him with the reeds of the *Ascraeus senex*, the old man of Ascra, i.e. Hesiod, with the clear implication that Gallus henceforth should direct his attention to composing didactic poetry in the Hesiodic mode beloved of the Alexandrians. Gallus wrote his didactic poem, but remained far better known for his four books of elegies addressed to Lycoris: Ovid *Amores* 3.9.63f., *Tristia* 4.10.53f. See further Boyle (1976) and Coleman (1977) *ad Ecl.* 6.64 and 72. On the literary issues raised in *Eclogue* 10, see Conte (1986), 126-29, and Loupiac (1993), 97.

[35] Cf Propertius 2.1, Ovid *Amores* 1.1, etc.

For them this is *segnitia* of the worst kind—debilitating, distracting, inefficient; *seruitium amoris* is inimical to *pietas* (which demands rather a *seruitium patriae*), and the well-run community has no time for this sort of frivolity. The issue is put very well by David Malouf in *An Imaginary Life*; the speaker is Ovid:

> The emperor has created his age. It is called Augustan, as our historians, with their eye fixed firmly on the present, have already announced. It is solemn, orderly, monumental, dull...
> I too have created an age. It is coterminous with his, and has its existence in the lives and loves of his subjects. It is gay, anarchic, ephemeral and it is fun. He hates me for it.[36]

The love-poet's vengeance on the agricultural and so *labor*-oriented god is signally appropriate: Orpheus destroys Aristaeus' bees.[37]

One final point. At the outset of this chapter, I referred to the fact that the first use of bees as an analogue of human social behaviour comes in the first extended simile of the *Iliad*. As *Georgics* 4 progresses, Homeric allusions become more and more evident,[38] culminating in the Aristaeus epyllion, with its manifest

---

36 Malouf (1978), 26.
37 On Aristaeus as a *labor* figure, see Davis (1979), 31f.; on Orpheus as a figure for the elegiac love-poet, see Conte (1986), 130-40. Perkell's (1978) suggestion that bees through their rejection of Venus have become 'guardians or symbols of chastity' (214) and therefore cannot survive under the tutelage of Aristaeus the rapist is interesting but ignores the fact that Proteus specifically points to Orpheus as the cause of their death (*has poenas Orpheus suscitat*, 454-56).
38 As may be seen at a glance by consulting the useful table in Wender (1979), 60. For Farrell (1991) it is more a case of saying that the Homeric allusions in

intertextual relationship with *Iliad* 1 and 18 and *Odyssey* 4. In the concluding lines of this epyllion Virgil even begins to ape Homer's way of narrating the fulfilment of instructions by using the same words *mutatis mutandis* in which the instructions were cast: Aristaeus' actions duplicate Cyrene's instructions in lines 550 (= 538), 551 (= 540, with the substitution of *ducit* for *delige*), 552 (= 544, with the substitution of *induxerat* for *ostenderit*) and 553 (which conflates 545 and 546).[39] This leads into a description of the new swarm of bees in which Virgil alludes to Homer's simile by incorporating the metaphor of a bunch of grapes: *uuam demittere* ('send down a cluster', 558) echoes βοτρυδόν ('in a cluster', *Il.* 2.89).[40] And this allusion to the opening of *Iliad* 2 is not the first we find in *Georgics* 4. I return to the passage I quoted at the outset:

> magnanimosque duces totiusque ordine gentis
> mores et studia et populos et proelia dicam.
>
> (*Georgics* 1.4f.)

---

the earlier books of the *Georgics* (and indeed in the first half of Book 4) are more subtle, whereas in the Aristaeus epyllion they are more overt—to the extent that, in Farrell's phrase, Virgil has incorporated 'Homeric raw material' (253). On the question of Homeric allusion in the *Georgics* see also Knauer (1981), 890-918.

[39] Griffin (1979) notes the repetition but not the obvious Homeric flavour.

[40] Knauer (1981), 900-03, argues against the notion that Homeric similes have 'influenced' the *narrative* of the *Georgics*. However this passage is a clear instance of narrative with Homeric simile as intertext—and a most significant simile at that. Oddly the allusion is not noted by Farrell, whose ear for such resonances is normally very acute. For another important instance of *Georgics* narrative alluding to Homeric simile see Thomas (1986), 178f. (*Georgics* 1.104-110~*Iliad* 21.257-62); here too the allusion importantly evokes the *context* of the original simile (the farmer in the act of irrigating being thus associated with Achilles fighting Xanthos/Skamandros).

> And I shall tell you of great-hearted leaders and of the
> customs, interests, communities and battles of an entire
> nation.

Magnanimus is the Latin equivalent of the Homeric epithet
μεγάθυμος; its use here in conjunction with *duces*, 'leaders'
evokes the μεγάθυμοι γέροντες, 'great-hearted elders', who
assemble by Nestor's ship to hear what Agamemnon has to say at
Iliad 2.53ff. These allusions at the beginning and conclusion of the
'book of bees' serve to remind us of the context in which Homer
employs his bee simile: the assembly of the Achaian forces to
which the simile refers comes about as a result of a false dream
sent to Agamemnon by Zeus, a dream which dangles before him
the promise of an immediate and successful outcome to the Trojan
expedition. And this is presented to us in a narrative in which
repetition, as in the conclusion to Virgil's Aristaeus narrative, is
particularly striking (what Zeus tells the dream is repeated by the
dream to Agamemnon who in turn repeats it to his council of
elders: 2.11-15 = 2.28-32 = 2.65-69). Octavian too has a vision for
the future: a quasi-bugonic regeneration of Rome from the
violence of civil conflict and a restoration of the values and the
mores that made Rome great. The fourth *Georgic* through its
Homeric allusion offers a timely reminder: any *anax*, *rex*, *princeps*
or *diui filius* with Olympian aspirations who thinks he can create
among human beings a regimented society like that of the bees is
the victim of delusion, a false dream. As the story of Orpheus
shows all too well, such visions are bound to founder on the rock
of intransigent human nature; unlike the bees, human beings are

indelibly subject to *amor*. And if you do not make a place for Orpheus, your bees will die anyway.[41]

And with that little handful of dust I conclude.

---

[41] Cf. Miles (1980), 289: 'It was Aristaeus' insensitivity to human loss and suffering that cost him his bees in the first place...Just as the farmer must understand the demands of nature and her inviolable laws, so equally must the statesman understand human nature and respect the essential tragedy of human life.' The juxtaposed images of the dying Cleopatra and the triumphant Caesar on Aeneas' shield in Book 8 of the *Aeneid* were to show the extent to which this *princeps* was capable of such an understanding.

BIBLIOGRAPHY

Austin, R.G. 1977. *P. Vergili Maronis Aeneidos Liber Sextus* (Oxford).

Barthes, R. 1982. *Selected Writings*, ed. S. Sontag (London).

Bishop, J.H. 1988. *The Cost of Power: Studies in the Aeneid of Virgil* (Armidale).

Block, E. 1980. 'Failure to Thrive: The Theme of Parents and Children in the *Aeneid* and its Iliadic Models', *Ramus* 9, 128-49.

Borges, J.L. 1970. *Labyrinths*, ed. D.A. Yates & J.E. Irby (Harmondsworth).

Boyle, A.J. 1976. *The Eclogues of Virgil* (Melbourne).

——— (ed.) 1979. *Virgil's Ascraean Song: Ramus Essays on the Georgics* (Berwick Victoria).

——— 1986. *The Chaonian Dove: Studies in the Eclogues, Georgics and Aeneid of Virgil* (Leiden).

——— (ed.) 1993. *Roman Epic* (London).

——— (ed.) 1995. *Roman Literature and Ideology: Ramus Essays for J.P. Sullivan* (Bendigo).

Bradley, A. 1969. 'Augustan Culture and a Radical Alternative: Vergil's Georgics', *Arion* 8, 347-58.

Brenk, F.E. 1992. 'The Gates of Dreams and an Image of Life: Consolation and Allegory at the End of Vergil's *Aeneid* VI', in Deroux (1992), 277-94.

Briggs, W.W. 1980. *Narrative and Simile from the Georgics in the Aeneid* (Leiden).

Camps, W.A. 1969. *An Introduction to Virgil's Aeneid* (Oxford).

Coleman, R. 1977. *Vergil: Eclogues* (Cambridge).

Conington, J. 1865. *The Works of Virgil with Commentary* (London).

Connor, P.J. 1979. 'The *Georgics* as Description: Aspects and Qualifications', in Boyle (1979), 34-58.

Conte, G.B. 1986. *The Rhetoric of Imitation: Genre and Poetic Memory in Virgil and Other Latin Poets*, ed. C.P. Segal (Ithaca & London).

Dahlmann, H. 1954. 'Der Bienenstaat in Vergils Georgica', *Akademie der Wissenschaft und der Literatur in Mainz, Abhandlungen der Geistes- & Sozialwissenschaftlichen Klasse* no. 10, 547-62.

Davis, P.J. 1979. 'Vergil's *Georgics* and the Pastoral Ideal', in Boyle (1979), 22-33.

Day Lewis, C. (tr.) 1966. *The Eclogues, Georgics and Aeneid of Virgil* (Oxford).

Deroux, C. (ed.) 1992. *Studies in Latin Literature and Roman History VI* (Brussels).

Di Cesare, M.A. 1974. *The Altar and the City: A Reading of Virgil's Aeneid* (New York and London).

Farrell, J. 1991. *Vergil's Georgics and the Traditions of Ancient Epic* (Oxford).

Feeney, D. 1986. 'History and Revelation in Vergil's Underworld', *Proceedings of the Cambridge Philological Society* 32, 1-24.

Goldberg, S.M. 1993. 'Livius and Naevius', in Boyle (1993), 19-36.

Gransden, K.W. 1984. *Virgil's Iliad: An Essay on Epic Narrative.* (Cambridge).

———— 1990. *Virgil: The Aeneid* (Cambridge).

Griffin, J. 1979. 'The Fourth *Georgic*, Virgil, and Rome', repr. in McAuslan & Walcot (1990), 94-111.

Haarhoff, T. 1960. 'The Bees of Virgil', *Greece & Rome* 7, 155-70.

Habinek, T.N. 1989. 'Science and Tradition in *Aeneid* 6', *Harvard Studies in Classical Philology* 92, 223-55.

Hardie, P. 1986. *Virgil's Aeneid: Cosmos and Imperium* (Oxford).

Harrison, S.J. (ed.) 1990. *Oxford Readings in Vergil's Aeneid* (Oxford).

Heinze, R. 1914. *Virgils epische Technik*[3] (Leipzig).

Horsfall, N.M. 1981. 'Virgil and the Conquest of Chaos', *Antichthon* 15, 141-50.

Johnson, W.R. 1976. *Darkness Visible: A Study of Vergil's Aeneid* (Berkeley and Los Angeles).

———— 1984. 'Vergil's Bees: The Ancient Romans' View of Rome', in Patterson (1984), 1-22.

Johnston, P. 1980. *Virgil's Agricultural Golden Age: A Study of the Georgics* (Leiden).

Joudoux, R. 1971 'La philosophie politique des "Géorgiques" d'après le livre IV (v. 149 à 169)', *Bulletin de l'Association Guillaume Budé*, 67-82.

Kenney, E.J. 1970. 'Doctus Lucretius', *Mnemosyne* 23, 366-92.

Klingner, F. 1967. *Virgil: Bucolica, Georgica, Aeneis* (Zürich).

Knauer, G.N. 1981. 'Vergil and Homer', *Aufstieg und Niedergang der Römischen Welt* II.31.2, 870-918.

Knight, D. 1991. 'Roland Barthes: An Intertextual Figure', in Worton & Still (1991), 92-107.

Kromer, G. 1979. 'The Didactic Tradition in Vergil's *Georgics*', in Boyle (1979), 7-21.

Lattimore, R. (tr.) 1968. *The Odyssey of Homer* (New York).

Leach, E.W. 1977. '*Sedes Apibus*: From the *Georgics* to the *Aeneid*', *Vergilius* 23, 2-16.

Loupiac, A. 'Le *labor* chez Virgile: essai d'interpretation', *Revue des Études Latines* 70, 92-106.

Luck, G. 1956. '*Studia Divina in Vita Humana*: On Cicero's "Dream of Scipio" and its Place in Graeco-Roman Philosophy', *Harvard Theological Review* 49, 207-18.

Lyne, R.O.A.M. 1994. 'Vergil's *Aeneid*: Subversion by Intertextuality', *Greece & Rome* 41, 187-204.

Malouf, D. 1978. *An Imaginary Life* (Woollahra).

McAuslan, I. & Walcot, P. (eds.) 1990. *Greece & Rome Studies: Virgil* (Oxford).

Michels, A.K. 1944. 'Lucretius and the Sixth Book of the *Aeneid*', *American Journal of Philology* 65, 135-48.

Miles, G. 1980. *Virgil's Georgics: A New Interpretation*. (Berkeley & Los Angeles).

Minyard, J.D. 1985. *Lucretius and the Late Republic: An Essay in Roman Intellectual History* (Leiden).

Mynors, R.A.B. 1990. *Virgil's Georgics* (Oxford).

Nadeau, Y. 1984. 'The Lover and the Statesman: A Study in Apiculture', in Woodman & West (1984), 59-82.

Nethercut, W.R. 1973. 'Vergil's *De Rerum Natura*', *Ramus* 2, 41-52.

Otis, B. 1964. *Virgil: A Study in Civilised Poetry* (Oxford).

Patterson, A.M. (ed.) 1984. *Roman Images: Selected Papers from the English Institute no. 8* (Baltimore).

Penwill, J.L. 1994. 'Image, Ideology and Action in Cicero and Lucretius', *Ramus* 23 (1994), 68-91.

Perkell, C.G. 1978. 'Virgil's Fourth *Georgic*', *Phoenix* 30, 211-21.

———— 1989. *The Poet's Truth: A Study of the Poet in Virgil's Georgics* (Berkeley & Los Angeles).

Powell, A. 1992. 'The *Aeneid* and the Embarrassments of Augustus', in *Roman Poetry and Propaganda in the Age of Augustus* (Bristol), 141-74.

Putnam, M.C.J. 1979. *Virgil's Poem of the Earth: Studies in the Georgics* (Princeton).

Reed, N. 1973. 'The Gates of Sleep in *Aeneid* 6', *Classical Quarterly* 23, 311-15.

Russell, D.A. 1979. 'De imitatione', in West & Woodman (1979), 1-16.

Segal, C.P. 1966a. '*Aeternum per saecula nomen*: The Golden Bough and the Tragedy of History' Part 2, *Arion* 5, 34-72.

59

———— 1966b. 'Orpheus and the Fourth *Georgic*', *American Journal of Philology* 87, 307-25.

Stehle, E.M. 1974. 'Virgil's *Georgics*: The Threat of Sloth', *Transactions of the American Philological Association* 104, 347-69.

Syme, R. 1960. *The Roman Revolution* (Oxford).

Thomas, R.F. 1986. 'Virgil's *Georgics* and the Art of Reference', *Harvard Studies in Classical Philology* 90, 171-98.

———— 1988. *Virgil: Georgics III-IV* (Cambridge).

———— 1991. 'The "Sacrifice" at the End of the *Georgics*, Aristaeus, and Vergilian Closure', *Classical Philology* 86, 211-18.

Tredennick, H., & Tarrant, H. (tr.) 1993. *Plato: The Last Days of Socrates* (Harmondsworth).

Wender, D. 1979. 'From Hesiod to Homer by Way of Rome', in Boyle (1979), 58-64.

West, D.A. 1987. 'The Bough and the Gate', repr. in Harrison (1990), 224-38.

———— & Woodman, T. (eds.) 1979. *Creative Imitation and Latin Literature* (Cambridge).

Williams, G. 1983. *Technique and Ideas in the Aeneid* (New Haven & London).

Williams, R.D. 1979. *Virgil: The Georgics* (New York).

———— 1985. *The Aeneid of Virgil: A Companion to the Translation of C. Day Lewis* (Bristol).

Wilkinson, L.P. 1969. *The Georgics of Virgil: A Critical Survey* (Cambridge).

———— (tr.) 1982. *Virgil: The Georgics* (Harmondsworth).

Wood, N. 1988. *Cicero's Social and Political Thought* (Berkeley and Los Angeles).

Woodman, T. & West, D. (eds.) 1984. *Poetry and Politics in the Age of Augustus* (Cambridge).

Worton, M. & Still, J. (eds.) 1991. *Intertextuality: Theories and Practices* (Manchester).

Zanker, P. 1988. *The Power of Images in the Age of Augustus* (Ann Arbor).

Zetzel, J.E.G. 1995. *Cicero: De Re Publica Selections* (Cambridge).

New from

AUREAL PUBLICATIONS

ROMAN LITERATURE AND IDEOLOGY:
RAMUS ESSAYS FOR J.P. SULLIVAN

edited

A.J. BOYLE

ISBN 0 949916 12 ...

[2000]   Rec. price $79.50

A collection of ten accessible essays published above covering a range of Roman literature from Catullus to Juvenal, together with an appreciation of Sullivan's own work. The collection explores Roman ideology in the relationship between ... and literature ... in Rome. In the manner in which it focuses ... in the display of ... such questions, Roman Literature and Ideology constitutes a worthy tribute to one who did so much to further the study of Roman literature.

Aureal Publications
PO Box 49
Bendigo North
Victoria
Australia 3550